THE Magnificent MIGRATION

THE Magnificent MIGRATION

On Safari with Africa's Last Great Herds

SY MONTGOMERY

with photos by Roger and Logan Wood

HOUGHTON MIFFLIN HARCOURT

BOSTON   NEW YORK

To the Estes family, with gratitude and love

hmhco.com

The text type was set in Bembo.
The display type was set in Northwell and Timberline.
Map art by Mike Reagan
Book design by Cara Llewellyn

Library of Congress Cataloging-in-Publication Data is on file.

ISBN: 978-0-544-76113-1

Printed in Malaysia
TWP 10 9 8 7 6 5 4 3 2 1
4500750885

Contents

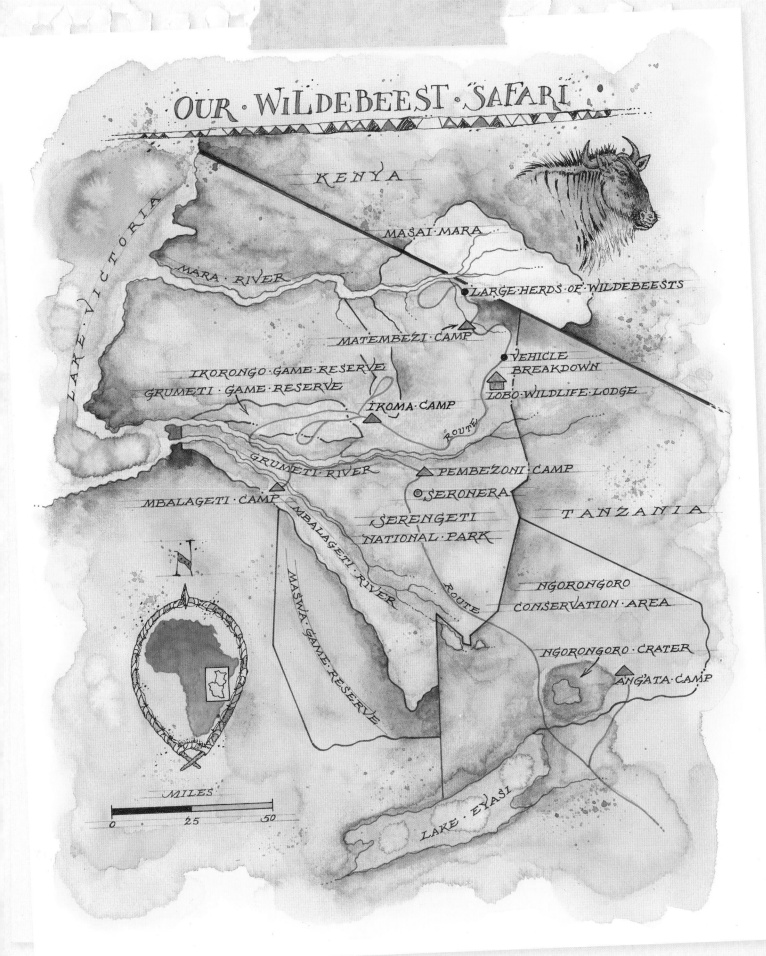

Lions aren't the only excitement in the Serengeti.

Chapter One

The grass is the color of lions. If the big cats weren't lying so close to the road, they'd be invisible. Thick manes frame two massive heads, marking them as adult males; the third is a lioness. Though their yellow eyes seem as indifferent as the sun, they are probably watching the same thing we are: a herd of fifty wildebeests about three hundred yards away from our Land Cruiser.

A nine-month-old calf cries plaintively: "Nyeh! Nyeh!" He's lost his mother. Though the adults pronounce it somewhat differently ("Neeh! Noo! Neeh! Noo!") the calf almost sounds like he's calling out the wildebeest's other common name: "Gnuuu! Gnnuuu!"

"If the lions notice the lost calf, they might become active," says wildlife biologist Dick Estes, the leader of our safari. But when one of the lions rises, it's a different drive he seeks to satisfy. He saunters over to the female and straddles her. He gives a few thrusts with his hips, but after five seconds, he gives up.

"I don't think they got it on," comments Liz Thomas. As a teen, she lived among lions in Namibia, and knows that lion lovemaking typically lasts longer than that—and ends with a swat and a snarl from the lioness. That's for good reason. The male has tiny barbs on his penis. But this lioness doesn't grumble; she flips over on her back, legs folded in the air, playful in the way of a sleepy puppy. The male returns to his other companion, who is probably his brother. He lies back down.

For now, the action is over. But other safari vehicles begin to gather. Lions are one of Africa's "big five" (the others are elephants, rhinos, Cape buffaloes, and leopards) that big-game hunters once sought as trophies, and that most tourists want to see today. Soon eleven cars are idling by the road.

"This is my nightmare," says Dick. "A crowd of vehicles watching lions do nothing, ignoring all the REAL excitement!"

Just past the lazing lions, the fifty wildebeests are engaged in dramas of life and death. They are advertising territory. They're seeking mates. They're finding the food that they need to sustain them on one of the greatest animal journeys on earth.

The lost calf reunites with his mother and rushes to her udder to suckle. A young bull

The "guru of gnu," DR. RICHARD DESPARD ESTES. Though he set his sights on Africa as a child, Dick took a circuitous route to get there. Graduating from Harvard in 1950 with a degree in sociobiology, he worked mainly as a writer till he got a chance to do a two-year survey of wildlife in Burma in 1958—where, among other adventures, a tiger investigated his tent one night. Upon his return to the United States, he enrolled at Cornell University for graduate school and proposed an ambitious multi-species study of five hoofed species of animals—elands, zebras, Thompson's and Grant's gazelles, and wildebeests—in Ngorongoro Crater. But wildebeests took up most of his time. They still do.

Dick has also conducted pioneering fieldwork on other antelope species, including years of study of the magnificent scimitar-horned sable and giant sable in Kenya and Angola. From 1978 to 2006 he chaired or cochaired the Antelope Specialist Group of the International Union for Conservation of Nature; he is a founding member and trustee of the Rare Species Conservatory Foundation, which designs protection and reintroduction programs for endangered species in the wild, and is especially proud that he helped repatriate the American-bred bongo, a beautiful striped antelope, to Kenya. But his heart belongs most of all to the wildebeests. For more than half a century, Dick has been acknowledged around the world as the wildebeest's most ardent and respected champion.

chases a rival, whose right horn was broken in combat. "There's so much going on!" says Dick.

But not many people know how to see it.

Dick does—and that's why we're here. My friend of thirty years, Dr. Richard Despard Estes has been studying these powerful, high-shouldered, bearded antelopes for more than half a century, longer than any other scientist who has ever lived.

From his white beard to his bush hat to his twinkling blue eyes, Dick looks as if he stepped out of Central Casting for the part of African wildlife biologist. The undisputed "guru of gnu," he's acknowledged the world over as *the* top expert on wildebeests. And though lions may seem more glamorous, it's wildebeests who drive the ecology and evolution of the largest savanna ecosystem in the world.

Like no other event in nature, the wildebeest migration defines wild Africa.

The extravagance of their number stupefies: one and a quarter million wildebeests, in separate herds of tens of thousands, all on the move at once, accompanied by hundreds of thousands of zebras and gazelles. It is the largest mass movement of animals on land.

The sheer number of so many animals in motion is more than a dazzling spectacle. It is a force like gravity, or rainfall—a force that transforms, nourishes, and renews both the lands over which they travel and the other creatures who gather in their wake.

The movements of the wildebeests are described in terms normally reserved for oceans or weather systems: They storm across rivers and lakes, dodging the jaws of crocodiles. They tumble down cliffs like waterfalls. They pour into the greening plains. The wildebeests follow the rains and the nourishing grasses in a roughly clockwise route of nearly a thousand miles, from Tanzania to Kenya, year-round. On their journey, they collect an unrivaled entourage of two hundred thousand zebras, five hundred thousand Thompson's gazelles, eighteen thousand elands, ninety-seven thousand topis—as well as the host of lions, leopards, jackals, hyenas, and vultures who eagerly await their arrival in their home territories.

"This is the greatest of all mammalian migrations," Dick tells me. "To be part of something that huge is an amazing feeling." And this is the quest that has drawn us here, on this Friday in late June, to Tanzania's Ngorongoro Crater. This is the gateway to Africa's great Serengeti plains, and part of the vast Serengeti–Masai Mara ecosystem of roughly twenty-five thousand square miles—the size of Connecticut and Rhode Island combined.

Our party of five has come from across the

United States to join Dick, eighty-eight, on what could be his last safari. We've come in hopes of finding the massive herds. We want to observe them during the wildebeests' chaotic and dramatic rut, or mating season. We hope to join them in taking part in the world's most magnificent animal migration.

"See that male?" Dick says, pointing to a tall, noble-looking young bull. The fringe of the gnu's long beard is backlit in the morning sun. "His head is up. He's not just standing around. He's doing three things: He's chewing the cud. He's watching for females and rival males. And he's advertising his territory."

Now, through his binoculars, Dick spots another, larger herd—perhaps several hundred animals. It's just a five-minute drive away from the cars still clotting around the lions. "Hot damn!" Dick says. We drive on.

It has taken us, it seems, a long time to see our first wildebeest of the trip. We've been on the move for four days.

We left the United States on Tuesday, cleared

Tanzanian customs at Kilimanjaro Airport on Wednesday, and after an overnight just outside Arusha city limits, we finally began—with several stops—the long drive toward Ngorongoro Crater on Thursday.

A finer group of traveling companions I could not imagine. Liz, eighty-five, lived in Africa for extended periods studying people and animals, and she's authored more than a dozen books. Gary Galbreath, sixty-six, a Chicago-based evolutionary biologist, has conducted research on animals on three continents. Roger Wood, fifty-three, a retired security software genius, and his son Logan, nineteen, from Portland, Oregon, have both traveled with Dick in the Serengeti before; the Woods have a summer home in New Hampshire not far from the Estes family, and Dick has taken three generations of Woods on safari with him. Logan made his first trip to Africa when he was only twelve; Roger has made seven previous journeys to Africa, several of them with Dick, assisting in his research.

On various writing projects, I've visited five African countries, including this one, but this is my first time in the Serengeti—and my only trip with Dick. I've wanted to go on this expedition with him for three decades, ever since my husband and I moved from New Jersey to New

ELIZABETH MARSHALL THOMAS, the author of a dozen acclaimed books, has spent a lifetime observing other creatures and other cultures, from the !Kung hunter-gatherers in Namibia, to the hidden lives of her dogs, to the deer in her backyard in New Hampshire. Liz and I met more than thirty years ago, shortly after I moved to the state. For a newspaper story, I interviewed her about her studies with Katy Payne on elephant infrasound. By the end of the interview we were fast friends. Liz introduced me to Dick and his wife, Runi, weeks later at a dinner at her house. The three of us have wanted to travel to Africa together ever since.

As a young woman, as well as living with the Bushmen of Namibia, Liz studied the lifeways of the Dodoth herders of Uganda. Here, some of her Dodoth friends examine some animal intestines, which they consult like the position of the stars, to determine whether a raid on their cattle might be coming.

ROGER WOOD thanks his mom, who loved travel, for knowing Dick. His parents lived not far from the Estes family. Roger's mom, Barbara, met Dick at his lecture on wildebeests at a local nature center in 1985; intrigued, Barbara soon joined Dick on safari. Roger met Dick at the Woods' summer cabin in New Hampshire, and they got to know each other and their families over many visits. In his work as senior director of product management for security software of McAfee/Intel (till his retirement in 2015), Roger looked for patterns—and that made him the perfect person to help Dick when he was looking for a field assistant in 1999. I'd heard about Roger from Dick for years. When we began planning our wildebeest safari, Dick and I knew we wanted Roger along—and we got his son Logan as a bonus!

LOGAN WOOD has a tattoo on his arm that says it all—in Arabic, a language he's been studying since high school. In the curving Arabic alphabet, it spells out "explore." With his parents and sister, Parker, Logan has visited a different country every year since fourth grade. When he's not scuba diving, skydiving, rock climbing, tightrope walking, or practicing archery, he's studying financial math and statistics at University of California, Santa Barbara.

GARY GALBREATH and I met in the Amazon in 1996. A seasoned field worker in the tropics and an ardent conservationist, when Gary wasn't teaching biology at Northwestern University or working at Chicago's Field Museum, he served on the board of the Rainforest Conservation Fund, which supported a reserve in Peru. I was there researching a book on pink dolphins. There he told me of a mysterious golden bear he'd seen years earlier in China, new to science. We later made three trips to Southeast Asia together to identify it. (It was an unknown color variant of the Asiatic black bear, or moon bear.) I wrote a book about it, and Gary has devoted years of study to its genetic lineage. Gary brought not only his long interest in Africa but also his extensive background in fieldwork and evolutionary biology to our wildebeest team.

Hampshire, to the town next to the one Dick (and Liz, who introduced us) lives in.

Dick literally wrote the book on African mammals. In fact, he wrote two: his field guides, *The Behavior Guide to African Mammals* and *The Safari Companion,* are considered so essential that it's almost impossible to find an English-speaking tourist group without one of them. Both books are used in training and certifying wildlife tour guides all over the African continent. And though his publisher wouldn't let him call his most recent book *The Gnu Testament* (instead they titled it *The Gnu's World*), it *is* considered the bible on the species.

Though we quickly left the city of Arusha

behind, it seemed to take forever to get to the wildebeests that Thursday. On our way to the Crater, we passed little shops known as *dukas* selling cakes and dresses; roadside nurseries selling orange-and-purple-flowered bird-of-paradise plants for the garden; coffee plantations, orchards of banana and coconut, and plots of corn and pigeon peas; and roadside stores with imaginative names like "Grand Slam Lubricant Shop."

We passed tall, yellow-barked fever trees—so-called because they grow in areas of standing water, breeding mosquitoes that spread diseases such as malaria. We stopped along the Mto wa Mbu, the "River of Mosquitoes," near

Lake Manyara National Park, where we viewed a rookery of yellow-billed storks. And we noted an intriguing sign posted near the entrance to the outer wall of the Rift Valley: Home to Tree-Climbing Lions.

We asked Dick, why do these lions climb trees?

"To escape biting flies," Dick answered. "It's a much more enticing sign than 'Home to a Boatload of Bloodsucking Flies.'"

All this time, we saw no wildebeests. But already, we had learned a lot: That in some areas, eagle owls eat almost nothing but hedgehogs. That tree hyraxes, which look like rodents but are closely related to elephants, descend from their treetop homes to deposit their dung in a common latrine. That if a cobra spits venom in your eye and you have no water, you should get someone to pee in it.

We learned that baobabs, the fat, squatty trees made famous by *The Little Prince,* are actually massive succulents, more like cacti than trees. They don't produce real wood or growth rings. The Hadza people, hunter-gatherers of Tanzania, say that the baobab angered God, so he plucked it from the earth and replanted it upside down.

Joshua Peterson, twenty-eight, at the wheel of our Land Cruiser, shared this last fact. His family operates Dorobo Safaris—Dorobo means "people without cattle"—and they have been leading camping and walking wilderness trips, often among the Hadza, since the early 1980s. Joshua's parents and uncles, brothers and cousins all know Dick, who has often headlined their trips as the featured naturalist. Joshua's parents were friends with Dick before Joshua was born. Joshua told me it was an "immense privilege" to be on this trip. "Dick doesn't just tell you what an animal is," Joshua said. "He knows what it's doing, why, and how it affects other animals."

As we drove west, toward the Crater, we each shared our stories. How did we all come to this distant land, a hemisphere away from home? Dick told us how he became fascinated with Africa at age ten. His family, driving from Memphis, Tennessee, to Dedham, Massachusetts, stopped at the American Museum of Natural History in New York City. There he saw the African dioramas in Akeley Hall: a cluster of eight taxidermied tuskers stand in its center, poised as if to charge, surrounded by twenty-eight life-size scenes from African plains and jungles. "On the spot," said Dick, "I decided I'd go to Africa." Today, at the famous Chicago Field Museum, there's a diorama of an African wildlife researcher's camp. It's based on Dick's campsite in Ngorongoro Crater, where he first started studying the wildebeest in 1962, and has a plaque about his work.

Liz had longed to visit Africa ever since reading *Jock of the Bushveld* as a child. At age eighteen, she got an extraordinary opportunity to do so. Her father, the founder of a successful national defense corporation, took the family to the uncharted Etosha Pan desert in Namibia, in southern Africa, to conduct some of the first-ever studies of hunter-gatherers. Liz's book on their life among the Bushmen, or San, became an instant classic, and *The Harmless People* is still in print today after nearly sixty years. Liz and her husband, Steve, later lived in Uganda when their two kids were small; after the kids were grown, she returned to Africa to collaborate with researcher Katy Payne on the landmark discovery that elephants use sounds below the threshold of human hearing to communicate across vast distances.

Roger, too, grew up reading books about Africa, and made sure both his kids—Logan and his younger sister, Parker—got to enjoy them as well. But for Gary, the trigger was a film. He was only six when he and his family saw the 1955 movie *The African Lion,* set in the Serengeti. He'd wanted to come ever since. In fact, more than forty years ago, he'd planned to research his PhD thesis on East Africa's colobus monkeys, but his funding fell through. He switched to studying armadillos in Florida, and became the world's top expert on the nine-banded species. Gary went on to teach biology at Northwestern University, earn an appointment at the Field Museum, and travel widely to study animals in South America and Southeast Asia. But he had never gotten to Africa. Until now.

Gary had been waiting the longest—sixty years. But by Thursday afternoon, all of us, af-ter three days of travel, felt increasingly eager to see at least one member of the great herds we hoped to follow.

At last we would get our chance, we hoped, when we reached the Crater View overlook point. A World Heritage site and an International Biosphere Reserve, Ngorongoro Crater is a natural sanctuary for almost all the large mammal species of East Africa's plains. We stood, chilly in the brisk wind even in our polar fleeces, at the lip of the Crater. We surveyed the panorama of the ancient volcano caldera below, ten by twelve miles in diameter: a mosaic of blue waterways and pale grasslands and dark trees. "This," Dick said, "is where I first looked down on the wildebeest as a graduate student from Cornell in 1962."

Before Dick's studies, the lives of the wildebeests were largely a mystery. Nobody knew much about which grasses they ate, how the young matured, how their social lives were organized, or how they affected their environment and the animals around them.

In fact, back then, nobody had more than a rough idea about where they went on their year-long migration. The technology of following animals with radio collaring was brand-new. The modern science of studying animal behavior, ethology, was only a decade old. Tanzania as an independent nation was then only one year old; formerly it had been governed by Germany, then by Great Britain. Native Tanzanians hadn't formally studied animals because few had the

Born in Nairobi, JOSHUA PETERSON grew up in the family business, Dorobo Safaris, sharing the wonders of African wildlife and culture with visitors from around the world. He's done his fair share of travel outside of Africa too: He went to college in Idaho (and spent his last year in New Zealand). After college he traveled further and worked for Idaho Fish and Game, studying how stocking fish in high mountain lakes affects the wild reptiles and amphibians. But Tanzania is his first love, and he loves to share it. Working with his dad, his uncle, and his two cousins, Joshua has been guiding for the past three and a half years. He spent 170 days on safari last year.

Joshua with a Masai friend, Alais, at Alais's "enkang" ceremony. An enkang is held every seven to nine years to celebrate the entry of young Masai men into the warrior age set. "My relationships with Alais and other Masai and Hadza have deepened my understanding of African wildlife and lifeways," explains Joshua. "Spending time in the bush with them, talking and telling stories around the fire, you get a very different perspective of animals and the bush—a nonscientific, more 'natural' understanding from people who live alongside the animals."

interest, education, or opportunity to do so.

Little was known about *any* African mammal. Jane Goodall's now-famous studies of chimps in Gombe had started only two years before. Few scientists were interested in studying wildebeests, even though—or perhaps because—they were the most numerous hoofed mammals in Africa.

But Dick suspected that these animals were more important than anyone else realized. Starting here, at this spot, Dick pioneered breakthrough after breakthrough in understanding the Serengeti's keystone species—a species that defines and sculpts the entire ecosystem. Meanwhile, the wildebeest brought Dick everything he loves.

Here, he met his wife, Runi, an Austrian who was in Tanzania working for a safari company. (The day after their wedding, they were back on the plains, observing the wildebeest calving season.) Their two children grew up in the Serengeti. Both kids now work in conservation. Son Lyndon is a conservation ecologist studying how climate change affects African ecosystems; daughter Anna, who will join us soon for part of our safari, studies African elephants by tracking

Dick's first tent in Ngorongoro.

Dick takes a primitive shower
at his first camp.

Later, Dick upgraded to this cabin
at the bottom of the Crater.

Dick and Runi as sweethearts on safari.

Dick and Runi's kids, Anna and Lyndon, grew up in the Serengeti. While their parents were taking data on wildebeests, they were watched by a babysitter, at left.

Dick prepares a sedative for the dart gun to radio collar a wildebeest.

Dick loads a dart gun in the early days of radio telemetry.

Dick releases a newly collared wildebeest.

them with radio collars, and works to prevent conflicts between people and animals.

Before becoming a wildlife biologist, Dick was a photojournalist for *Yankee Magazine*. He spent two years writing a book about the social and natural history of the East Coast, and then two years on a wildlife survey of Burma. Though all valuable pursuits, compared with what he found with the wildebeests, to Dick, these accomplishments were nothing. "I wasted my life before I made plans to go to Africa," Dick insisted. "Then my life began."

As Dick did on his first trip here more than fifty years before, standing on the lip of the Crater, we raised binoculars to our eyes to scan the vast area two thousand feet below. The little black dots on the lion-colored plain below were probably 1,500-pound African Cape buffaloes, Dick told us. "It's like looking over a whole world," I said.

"Yes, it's a microcosm," Dick replied. The Crater is a sort of Serengeti in miniature, enclosed by the walls of the extinct volcano whose caldera is now grassland. But, like the rest of the Serengeti ecosystem, and all of Africa, the Crater is a world rapidly changing. Introduced foreign plants are taking hold where native grasses once flourished. Poachers threaten its rhinos and elephants. Masai herders' cattle, goats, and sheep compete with native animals to graze. Climate change skews annual rainfall. Four hundred and fifty thousand tourists visit the Crater each year, their vehicles compacting soil and carving ruts

into the grasses. And every year, more houses, roads, and businesses crowd closer to the park's boundaries.

Throughout the Serengeti, our kind threatens the very survival of the migration we've come so far to witness.

———

We'd been gazing at the plain below for half an hour when at last, at 5:04 p.m. that Thursday, Dick was the first to spot a wildebeest. Just one.

Where were the teeming herds? Were they

gone already? That's what Dick thought in 1962. He saw one lone wildebeest—and then, a bit of distance away, another loner. "I thought, 'Those must be territorial males,'" he said. "And so it turned out." He had, in a glance, understood a key aspect of the wildebeest's social world. During the mating season, the migratory mature bulls hold small territories that they advertise and defend until the females stream out of the area.

I marveled at Dick's insight back then—and his sharp vision at age eighty-eight. Even with binoculars that magnify an image ten times, I couldn't tell the wildebeest apart from the other black dots, which were Cape buffaloes. One dot, which Roger spotted, was a critically endangered black rhino. I stared and stared through the field glasses—but the rhino, like the wildebeest, still looked like a shapeless dot to me.

It isn't until now, on this chilly Friday morning, that we find ourselves actually driving through the Crater—and have the wildebeests clearly in our sights. Now, at last, I feel the trip I have awaited for three decades has finally begun.

Ngorongoro Crater: the Serengeti in miniature.

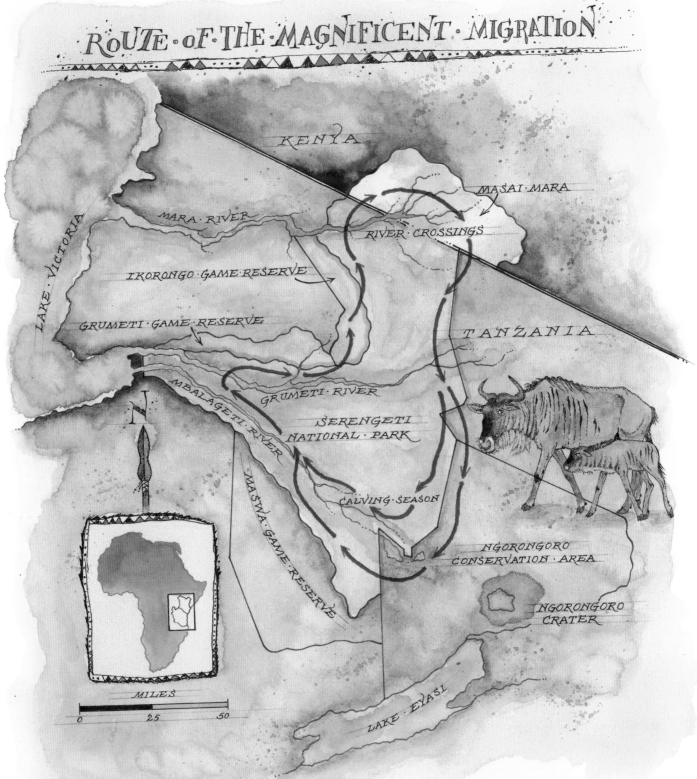

ROUTE·OF·THE·MAGNIFICENT·MIGRATION

KENYA

MASAI·MARA

MARA·RIVER

RIVER·CROSSINGS

LAKE·VICTORIA

IKORONGO·GAME·RESERVE

GRUMETI·GAME·RESERVE

TANZANIA

N

MBALAGETI·RIVER

GRUMETI·RIVER

SERENGETI
NATIONAL·PARK

MASWA·GAME·RESERVE

CALVING·SEASON

NGORONGORO
CONSERVATION·AREA

NGORONGORO
CRATER

MILES

0   25   50

LAKE·EYASI

Migration Without End

ROBINS FLY SOUTH IN THE WINTER, NORTH IN THE SPRING. HUMPBACK WHALES feed for months in Arctic waters, then swim to breed in the tropics. The migrations we commonly think of are twice-yearly events: animals leave a summer home for a distant winter one, stay awhile, and then go back again. Their trips are dramatic, swift marathons, like that of the amazing bar-tailed godwit. This large, long-billed, long-legged wading bird completes its nonstop flight of seven thousand miles from Alaska to New Zealand in nine or ten days.

The migration of the Serengeti wildebeests is different. Theirs isn't a rapid movement between two seasonal ranges. Chasing the rains and the most nourishing grasses, theirs is a year-round, clockwise journey whose route traces a shape like a child's drawing of a head facing west with a big nose sticking out. They travel from Kenya's Masai Mara south to Tanzania, west and north across the Serengeti Plains, and north to Kenya again. Each year they cover more than eight hundred miles, the equivalent of circumnavigating Britain and Ireland. But, although the gnus may linger in one spot for days, their migration has no endpoint; it's a cycle. Even during the calving season, when hundreds of thousands of mothers give birth to their young, the herd is on the move—which is why wildebeest calves, unlike any other antelope, can stand at the tender age of seven *minutes*, and keep up with their fleet mothers within two days.

Also, the route, while always similar, isn't always the same each year. Wildebeests who inundated one area one year might not even show up there the next. Sometimes they don't even go in the "right" direction; wildebeests are known to reverse direction, sometimes for miles.

And contrary to the TV shows you've seen, showing rivers of stampeding gnus, the migration is, more often than not, a much more leisurely affair. (One reason they're running on TV: the filmmakers in helicopters overhead frighten them.) Much of the time, migrating wildebeests are in no great rush. In good years, between the short rainy season from November through December and the longer rainy season of April and May, pastures remain green for weeks on end. Wildebeests may not need to travel more than a few miles a day. But when there is little or no rain, usually from June through October, the emerald of the short-grass plains gives way to pale tan. The gnus pick up the pace. In search of graze and water, they can travel fifty miles a day. When a wildebeest is really in a hurry (with a lion or cheetah on his heels) one can gallop more than forty miles an hour, nearly ten miles an hour faster than a running white-tailed deer.

Though the Serengeti wildebeests' year-round trek is the world's largest and most famous land migration, long, traditional, regular animal journeys have been going on since at least the Jurassic. From the elements in teeth shed by dinosaurs 150 million years ago, scientists know that the giant plant-eating sauropods of North America made regular, seasonal journeys from low to high ground to escape drought and avoid food shortages. Fossils show that three hundred thousand years ago, extinct pouched mammals that looked like giant wombats once made regular treks across the continent of Australia.

From tiny microorganisms to whales, from birds to reptiles, from dragonflies to fish, many different kinds of animals around the world today are on the move, traveling from one home to another, to take advantage of a particular location's special opportunities for food, for breeding, or for safety.

Like the wildebeests, these migrants' coordination can seem symphonic; their movements, at times, explosive. But what may be overlooked in the dazzle of all this movement is that these animals' migrations, too, are a massive, driving force that surely impacts everything around them: the land, the water, the plants, their predators, and their prey.

In each case, migrating animals change, nourish, and renew the vast areas over which they move. The stories of their travels are epics, full of drama, adventure, beauty, and tragedy—some of which scientists are only now starting to record, and many of which researchers don't yet understand. You'll find other examples of magnificent migrations highlighted in these pages as you read on.

Territorial male on his stomping ground.

On migration, plains zebras are considered pioneers for the wildebeests.

Chapter Two

Animals are everywhere we look. To one side, a herd of about fifty zebras. To the other, a family of warthogs—the proud, tusked mom followed by four babies. They trot briskly with slender, tufted tails aloft. Ahead, a pool is packed with hippos. In the distance, Liz spots a hyena. My friends' reports echo all around me:

"Look, an ostrich!"

"I see another lion."

"What raptor is that?"

The wildebeest herd Dick has spotted appears to number about four hundred. But almost immediately, Dick sees an even larger group only a minute's drive away. Slowly, respectfully, Joshua drives on to approach them, sticking to the track. He kills the motor.

"I'd say we're close to a thousand here," says Dick.

And soon, as if our vehicle weren't even there, they are all around us.

Wildebeests are grazing only ten yards away—near enough for me to see, with the naked eye, two swollen ticks in one's ear. Some are nibbling grass, some are strolling, some stand, heads held high, looking around. Here and there, a few canter about. Everyone is calling "Neh! Noo! Neh! Noo! Neh! Noo!"

"This is astonishing!" says Gary, awestruck.

We feel as if we have been suddenly transported inside one of the American Museum of Natural History's African dioramas—or perhaps inside the one featuring Dick's campsite at the Field Museum. Granted, our sleeping quarters here are considerably more comfortable than those Dick enjoyed when he first arrived: for his first six months on the Crater floor, he lived in a canvas British Army tent from World War II, pitched beneath a grove of fig trees. It was sometimes raided by baboons and occasionally visited by leopards. (Later he built a safer, twelve-by-eighteen-foot cabin on the same site.)

We are staying in tents, too, but our camp

A male ostrich flushes pink to attract a mate.

on the Crater's rim is deluxe. Each spacious, private tent is really a suite, with lights provided by generator and a private attached bath where we can even take a hot shower—poured into an overhead bucket outside by attentive staff.

But even in these luxurious accommodations, I'm struggling with the same questions that Dick faced when he first showed up to study the wildebeests:

How to make sense of it all? Who's who, and what are they doing?

Dick shows us how to tell the sexes apart. (They're called bulls and cows, like cattle.) It's more difficult than you might think. Both sport the same brown-and-black coat, white beards, black manes, and cow-like, upturned horns. However, the adult males' horns grow longer and thicker than the females'. (In both sexes, the gap between the two horns widens with age.) But, as Dick explains, during the rut, it's the animals' behavior that really sets the sexes apart.

"The ones directly around us are bach-

Excited, a bull displays on hind legs to a cow.

elor males," Dick explains. About half of all adult males are bachelors, who were not able to win the competition with other bulls to establish and hold territories. That's why they're bachelors. Without real estate, they're unlikely to attract the attention of any females. So the bachelors hang out together, sometimes by the dozen, sometimes in the hundreds or more, as they travel on migration. Sometimes they'll spar with their horns, but mainly it's just for fun. If a territory becomes available, a bachelor will try to claim it. But even though territorial male wildebeests will tolerate closer spacing than any other antelope, there are just not enough suitable spots for every male to hold a territory.

It's the rutting bulls who cause the colossal commotion that Dick calls "the Big Hum." This deafening chorus is the soundtrack of the rut. All the bulls, whether they've secured a territory or not, are calling their hearts out, amid a frenzy of herding, chasing, showing off, and fighting as they compete with one another to try to round up, detain, and mate with cows. "It's nonstop mayhem!" Dick tells us.

No wonder. It seems that as migrants, territorial bulls have set themselves an almost impossible task: How can they hold a territory and migrate at the same time? How can they persuade any of the cows to drop out of the journey long enough to stay with them? And how can they detain and corral the cows while fighting off all the rivals who want to horn in?

We hope we'll soon see. "Our purpose today is to get views and pictures of rutting behavior," Dick says. But at first, it seems that nothing much is going on.

With her binoculars, Liz spies a lone wildebeest in the distance. "A wildebeest all by himself!" she says. "It's heartbreaking. He's a social species, and he's all alone. He's trying to attract females, and he's unsuccessful."

"Oh, but he's *not* unsuccessful," says Dick. "He's just waiting for a female to come into his territory."

This bull is showing off for an audience that has yet to notice him. Standing tall on a small patch of dirt bared by his hooves and strewn with his dung, known as his "stamping ground," he cuts a handsome figure indeed: his deep chest, short neck, and high shoulders radiate power and confidence. At rest, he seems as still as a soldier guarding Buckingham Palace. He might not move off his stamping ground for a full hour.

Instead of a palace, he's guarding his patch of grass—an area smaller than a suburban backyard. Standing there, he's sending out two messages at once. To males: keep off. To females: come hither. His real estate, and not his physique or personality, is what he's advertising to the ladies: "Look! Delicious grass. Close proximity to water. Fine views to spot predators." If they like it, maybe they'll stick around long enough to come into season, and let him mate with them, before they move on.

Dick's studies show that the average territorial bull spends 80 percent of the rut with no cows on his territory at all! But though they look lonely, they're not really alone. Dick discovered, in the course of his doctoral thesis research, that the territorial bulls engage with their closest neighbors in an elaborate challenge ritual every day.

For anywhere from a few moments to up to forty-five minutes, neighboring gnus, typically 140 feet apart, will approach one another, side on, heads raised. For a few minutes, they may graze almost face-to-face. Then they check each other's chemistry. One usually defecates or urinates, and the other grimaces—but not in distaste. The other male is exposing the vomeronasal organ in the roof of his mouth so he can chemically analyze the other bull's hormones. As Dick explains it, as the rival male curls his upper lip, he's challenging his neighbor, "Show me that your testosterone level is worthy of holding a territory!"

Sometimes the two males cavort; sometimes they kneel, in combat position; sometimes they clash horns. Or, sometimes they both just lie down together. And then, suddenly, they seem to agree that their daily chore is completed. They both get up and go back to standing tall on their stamping grounds, hoping for females to come by.

The territorial bulls also get visits from other species. Thompson's and Grant's gazelles, zebras, and others may join them on their territory. "And these bulls leave their territory to drink,

Territorial bull wildebeests clash horns.

and meet other wildebeests there," Dick says. "They're not as isolated as you might think."

We move on, and soon we come to a new group—where several territorial males are having more success than the lone guy we just saw. Each bull has attracted a group of cows. But each covets the ladies on his neighbor's property. One large bull chases another—who then rushes into the territory of a third. "The first guy is acting like a billiard ball, setting off the other ones!" says Gary.

"He's acting properly for a rutting bull," replies Dick, with a trace of shared male pride. The first bull returns to his territory and walks up to one of the five cows hanging out with him. She's sitting, resting, and chewing the cud. He nudges her with his nose. She obligingly rises at his urging. "If she's in estrous, she'll let him know," Dick says. If she's ready to mate, she'll urinate, and using the vomeronasal organ in the roof of his mouth, the bull will be able to detect the hormones that signal he could father her next calf.

But the cow doesn't urinate, and the bull gets the message. Not today. But if he can keep her on his territory just a little longer . . .

Josh drives on, looking for more rutting action. We watch some young males playfully sparring with one another. Dick identifies one as a big two-year-old, and the other one as about three. The bigger one drops to his knees, and then so does the other. With lowered heads, they shake their horns. The elder rubs his head in the dirt. The two touch horns. They part, stand, kneel again, paw the earth. "This is play," Dick explains. "They're just having a good time."

This is nothing like the fights Dick has witnessed when females are at stake. Bulls determine dominance by combat. Sometimes they will simply run and ram invaders—so hard that the impact can break a horn, and wildebeest horns are tough enough to deflect an axe blow.

"I wonder when these chaps will be gearing up for the rut?" asks Dick.

Soon we encounter a herd of females with calves. The little ones, with inch-long spike horns, closely follow their mothers, usually at their sides, partially concealed by the curtain of their mothers' beards. They all seem about the same size. That's because they're remarkably close in age: 80 percent of the Serengeti ecosystem's six hundred thousand wildebeest calves are born during a brief three-week period just before the rainy season—so many that the hyenas, lions, leopards, and wild dogs cannot possibly eat them all.

Though these calves look healthy, Dick is unsettled. "These calves don't look four months old," he says. They're too small.

Usually, in the Crater, the calves are born in February—a little earlier here than the rest of the Serengeti ecosystem. The rut starts four months later. But while the rut is an annual ritual, it doesn't always happen at the same time. "It can be as much as a month early or late," Dick warns us. And by the look of these calves,

This newborn will grow spike horns within weeks.

this year the births—and the timing of the rut—have been significantly delayed.

The timing of the wildebeests' life cycle will change with drought or flood. It will change if rains come early or late. It will change if herders' livestock have overgrazed the plains in the migration's usual path. It will change with the decisions people make about when to burn the grasses to encourage fresh growth—which herders have done here for thousands of years, and a practice that park managers continue today.

These factors always make everything about these antelopes' lives unpredictable. But it's even more so now. Global climate change is disrupting seasons all over the world. On top of that, this is an El Niño year. Occurring about once every two to seven years, a natural upwelling of warm, nutrient-rich waters off the coasts of Peru and Ecuador weakens the equatorial trade winds flowing from east to west over the Pacific Ocean and changes weather around the globe. In East Africa, El Niño can cause both flood *and* drought. It may well have affected the calving season—and if so, that will change the timing of the rut.

A year ago, when we planned this safari, Dick drew upon more than half a century of experience to try to time our trip to coincide with the wildebeests' mating season. But with so many variables, we knew, even back then, that our timing could be off. It was possible we'd miss the rut.

What I did not fully realize until now was that the same variables that affect the rut also affect the timing—and the route—of the entire migration.

On top of the usual unknowns, El Niño and global climate change could put the objective of our safari in jeopardy. The bulk of the Serengeti's great wildebeest herds may have already left.

We could, I realized with growing dismay, miss the whole thing.

This infant will be able to run at the tender age of seven minutes old.

What Is a Wildebeest?

DEEP-CHESTED, SHORT-NECKED, HIGH-SHOULDERED, AND THIN-LEGGED: THE wildebeest, goes the joke, looks like it was created by committee. Others insist that with its goat-like beard, cow-like horns, and horse-like mane, it must have been made out of spare parts.

But if that's so, the committee must have been a smart one, and used all the *best* parts. "How else, then, could wildebeests be so successful that they outnumber everybody else by hundreds to one?" Dick likes to ask.

The wildebeest is the most abundant antelope in all of Africa—the continent most richly blessed with antelope species, boasting seventy-five different kinds. (America,

by comparison, has none. The pronghorn isn't an antelope, and in fact is more closely related to giraffes!)

All antelopes have horns. These are hard, permanent, bony growths—unlike antlers, which are made of the same stuff as fingernails and are grown and then shed each year. Antelopes all have cloven hooves and special four-chambered stomachs. Like their domesticated relatives, the sheep, goats, and cattle, antelopes all chew the cud. They grab grass with their lower teeth and upper gums, swallow it, and move on. Hours later, they burp it back up again and chew in a distinctive side-to-side motion. Why eat your food twice? Because grass isn't very nutritious. The antelopes' four-part stomach evolved to glean nutrients from a diet few other animals can stomach.

But the wildebeest is not just another antelope; it's one of the most highly evolved and unusual antelopes in the world, Dick explains. "They're perfectly adapted to the ecology of the area," Dick says. "The wildebeest is the perfect fit for where it lives."

There are two separate species, and five distinct subspecies, of wildebeest, all of them in Africa. They are also all called gnus—though Dick notes that only the black wildebeests, native to southern Africa, actually pronounce their own name that way. Of them all, only the western white-bearded wildebeest still thrives in immense migratory herds. These are the ones we hope to follow as they sweep across the Serengeti plains.

Everything about the animal seems built to withstand the rigors of migration. Its high shoulders slope down to lower hindquarters. Hyenas have this body shape, too. It's a configuration that's energetically efficient for long-distance travel, especially at a canter, with its easy, three-beat gait. The wildebeests' dark color makes them stand out from most other antelopes. They sport reverse countershading—dark below and lighter above—which Dick notes "makes them even more conspicuous than the zebra" and thus makes it easier for them to stick together on their trek. Secretions from glands in the hooves help them follow each other by scent, even in the dark. The nostrils have flaps that filter dust kicked up by thousands of migrating animals. Even the infants are equipped for travel from the start. Unlike all other antelopes, whose mothers hide them in tall grass for weeks or months after birth, gnu babies move along with the herd from the day they're born.

Another Magnificent Migrant: The Arctic Tern

THIS WHITE-AND-BLACK SEABIRD WINS THE distance award for longest migration on earth. Each bird flies a zigzagging route of forty-four thousand miles from pole to pole—an aerial path that scientists discovered in 2010 was twice as long as previously thought.

Tiny, lightweight transmitters attached to a band on birds' legs recently revealed that these four-ounce featherweights edged out another, bigger bird—the sooty shearwater, seven times its weight—as the world's longest-distance migrant by a whopping four thousand miles.

And since the arctic tern can live more than thirty years, over its lifetime, a bird might migrate 1.5 million miles. That's equivalent to three trips to the moon and back.

Researchers were surprised to discover that, on their way to their wintering grounds along the shores of Antarctica's Weddell Sea, the birds often stop for a month and float on the waves in the open North Atlantic Ocean. Scientists suspect they are tanking up on rich supplies of fish and small crustaceans here before setting off to cross the tropics.

Arctic terns also zigzag back during their spring migration to their Greenland breeding grounds in the Arctic. Instead of traveling straight up the middle of the Atlantic, the birds fly from Antarctica to Africa, then to South America, and from there on to the Arctic.

That's quite a detour—one scientists never suspected. But it makes sense. The tiny transmitters suggest the birds are following huge spiraling wind patterns in the atmosphere, avoiding flying into the wind.

Zebras prefer long, tough grass stems, leaving shorter grasses for the wildebeests.

Chapter Three

Dick is right. The rut, at least in the Crater, is late.

After a morning cruising the Crater floor, we stop at the cool, misty rim of the research station to visit one of Dick's many fellow scientist friends. Ingela Jansen, a Swede, is studying Ngorongoro's seventy resident lions, keeping tabs on them with camera traps (which snap animals' photos when they approach) and telemetry collars (which track animals' movements with signals emitted from the collar to overhead satellites). And yes, she confirms, she noticed that the wildebeest calves were born a month late this year.

Ingela's news about the rut is distressing.

"Don't worry!" Anna Estes reassures us. Dick's elephant researcher daughter joined us at our camp the night before. "What's going on in the Crater," she says, "may not be the case for the rest of the wildebeests in Serengeti."

Though Ngorongoro Crater is part of the immense Serengeti ecosystem, in another sense,

In contrast to the Crater floor, the rim of Ngorongoro is cool and misty, the trees festooned with moss.

ANNA ESTES. Growing up in Serengeti, Anna's favorite friends (besides her brother, Lyndon, who is two and a half years older) were mongooses and hyraxes—small mammals of the African plains. Though she spent her later childhood in New England, she returned to Africa to research her PhD in environmental science, satellite collaring and tracking elephants to study how human activities affected their lives. Today she lives and works in Tanzania, supervising graduate students' field studies of African wildlife through the Nelson Mandela African Institution of Science and Technology in Arusha.

Anna's older brother, Lyndon, works in conservation too. Here he is with a sedated lion.

it's a world unto itself. Since it's an extinct volcano, the Crater's soils are more fertile than elsewhere in the Serengeti. Its diversity of grasses is so rich it can support a large wildebeest population that may not ever have to leave its giant bowl. These roughly ten thousand gnus typically rove through the Crater's 117 square miles on their own mini-migration throughout the year. But under certain conditions—like when the rains are delayed—up to a third of the Crater's wildebeests may leave, escaping over the volcano's western wall to join the larger Serengeti population on their trek.

Outside Ngorongoro's volcano walls, the wildebeest rut might well be just starting. It could already be in full force. Or it could also be delayed. It could even be early. With cell phone and internet service spotty, the only way to tell will be to find the migrating masses and see. That is, *if* we can find them.

Fortunately, we'll have help. This is a busy time of year for visitors hoping to see the migration, and wherever we camp, whenever we stop in the road, Dick and Anna converse in Swahili or English with the drivers and guides about where they've seen large herds of wildebeests. Almost all of them are carrying Dick's *Safari Companion,* and many of them recognize him as the author and stop him for an autograph.

Anna brings news that, two weeks ago, Serengeti National Park authorities set fire to the dry grasses along the area ahead of us, known as the Western Corridor, to encourage new growth. "And since then," she adds, "they've had some good rains."

"It's possible the wildebeests pushed ahead," Dick says—to take advantage of the first flush of green grass. This is important intelligence. Tomorrow, we'll check in with three of Dick's scientific colleagues who should be able to help us locate the big herds with more accuracy.

But in the meantime, whether we catch up with the great herds or not, we will nevertheless be feeling their impact. We will be traveling in the world that the wildebeests created. "Where the migration goes defines the Serengeti ecosystem," Dick reminds us. And that definition is literal: the United Nations, when it refers to the Serengeti ecosystem, does so not by any geographic borders, but as *the area covered by the wildebeest migration.*

The Serengeti itself was sculpted by the gnus' endless circular trek. Its grasses are cropped by their teeth, enriched by their manure, churned by their hooves. During the rut, aggressive males bash small bushes and saplings with their horns, using them like punching bags; Dick's research has shown that this also keeps the sa-

Lahai acacia trees draped with beards of lichen at the Crater's rim at dawn.

vanna open, preventing bush from encroaching. Even a component in the gnus' saliva has been found to nourish the grass they graze. (A similar natural chemical has been found in the saliva of North America's bison, whose great migration, before settlers decimated the buffaloes, rivaled that of today's Serengeti wildebeests.)

"The fact that they migrate enables twenty-eight species to share the Serengeti," Dick explains. "If the wildebeests didn't migrate, they'd eat the other herbivores out of house and home. But instead, they create the conditions for these other species to thrive."

Not only do other herbivores benefit. So do the ten large predators, from lions to hyenas, who hunt the herbivores. And so do the scavengers, like the vultures and the dog-like jackals, who feast on the remains that predators leave behind. To a large extent, all the animals we'll meet along the way owe their lives to the wildebeest migration. Their story is also the story of the wildebeests.

We leave our misty, chilly camp shortly after dawn. A salmon sunrise peeks beneath white and silver clouds as we descend from the forest. As the altitude drops, the temperature rises, and soon we find ourselves in a different ecosystem

A lion and lioness trudge by our vehicle like weary commuters.

completely. Great, flat-topped lahai acacia trees draped with beards of pale-green lichen give way in minutes to the dry, tan grass on the Crater floor. The altitude change—from 7,500 feet to 5,900 feet—is so dramatic my ears pop.

Today we'll traverse the Crater, heading over its northwest rim, to the Serengeti plains. "This could be our best chance to get up close and personal with wildebeests!" Dick announces hopefully.

But almost as soon as we reach the Crater floor, we're stuck in a small traffic jam. Three other vehicles are stopped in the track. Two adult lions, a male and a female, plod by, right beside the cars. They look as bored and weary as tired commuters. We stop and stare in wonder as the lions come almost close enough to touch.

"Let's go somewhere there are more animals," Dick says indignantly, "like the wildebeests we're supposed to be looking for."

Joshua drives on, but soon we must stop again. Our journey is interrupted by another: a line of plains zebras, stretching as far as the eye can see.

"Look at that!" says Roger, amazed even though he's seen it before. "Wow!" says Gary, raising his camera. "I've never seen so many animals!"

They flow across the road purposefully, single file, as orderly as polite grade-schoolers in

Often zebras head in the same direction as wildebeests.

line. With a glance, Dick knows what's happening. These zebras have spent the night sleeping on the shortest, most open grasslands. While the others napped—adults on folded legs, foals sprawled on their sides—at least one herd member stood guard. Now they are moving to their grazing grounds in taller pastures.

Often wildebeests join zebras, heading in the same direction. On migration, the plains zebras are considered pioneers for the wildebeests; though the zebras are only two-thirds as efficient at extracting protein from their food (because they lack the wildebeests' four-chambered stomach), the striped horses can eat long, tough stems the wildebeests cannot. Trampling and cropping the taller grasses, the zebras reveal the shorter species of grasses, between one and four inches high, that the wildebeests prefer.

Though wildebeests and plains zebras often migrate together, their herds are very different, Dick explains. "This huge group of zebras is composed of both harem herds and bachelor herds," he says. The leader of a harem is always an experienced mare, followed in line by her young offspring, followed by the other mares and their young offspring. A stallion, who defends against predators, brings up the rear. Even if their stallion kicks out their adolescent male offspring, even if their stallion is deposed by a stronger male, the harem females stay together for life.

The other grouping is the bachelor herd, up to seventeen males, five years old or older. Even

while on migration, zebra herds maintain their group unity. The important thing is this: "Everyone knows everyone else," Dick explains.

But that's not the case with migratory wildebeests. Dick is, in fact, the one who figured this out. He wondered whether wildebeests had "besties"—friends or relatives who stick together during their yearly travels. When radio collars became available, he used the tracking devices to follow migrating bachelor wildebeests who he noticed hanging out together. Did they stay together on the long trek? They did not. The same was the case with the females. "Except for mothers and their calves or yearlings," he explains, "everyone's a stranger."

I'm staggered. It sounds horrible! It reminds me of my first day of fifth grade: I was a shy kid who had just moved to a new school in a new town in a new state. I remember moving from one classroom to the next, caught in a throng of noisy strangers in the hallway, not knowing anyone. I hated it.

Do the migrating wildebeests feel that way? "Not at all," says Dick. Wildebeests are incredibly social. In his *Behavior Guide to African Mammals,* Dick described wildebeests as "among the most gregarious and socially advanced" of all the hoofed animals on earth. They're the sort of souls who can walk into a crowded party full of strangers and feel safe. As long as they're with other wildebeests, they're less likely to be picked off by a predator. They love company—the more the merrier.

These super-social beasts are happy to hang out with lots of other kinds of creatures as well. Some of their most frequent traveling companions are in sight right now, opposite the filing zebras: slender, cinnamon-and-white gazelles with a single, bold stripe on each side and ridged, parallel horns.

"Grant's!" calls Gary—and at the same moment, Logan calls "Thompson's!"

Both men are right. But I can't tell: Which gazelle is which?

People often have trouble telling these two species of graceful antelopes apart. They not only range the same plains, but also mingle in the same herds. It's not uncommon to find a male in a female herd of the other species! One species always has a side stripe, and the other does sometimes. But the gazelles don't get con-

This adult male Grant's gazelle lacks the black side stripe, though females and young often sport them.

fused—and neither does Dick. There are several ways to tell one from the other. For example, the Grant's is larger, but that doesn't always help. Is it a big male Thompson's or a young female Grant's?

Dick shows us a sure trick: "Look at the animal's tail!" The black tail of the Thompson's gazelle just can't stay still. It twitches like a piano metronome on steroids, sweeping back and forth across a white rump patch. The tail tells a tale, Dick explains: "They're saying, 'I'm a Tommy! I'm a Tommy! I'm a Tommy!'" The Grant's gazelle just yards away, by contrast, has a white tail, and it hardly moves at all. The tail twitching probably evolved as a way to help the two species keep straight who's who at a glance, Dick reckons.

Where do these antelopes fit in along the wildebeest migration? As zebras chomp the taller grasses and reveal the understory for the wildebeests, the wildebeests pay the favor forward. They crop the medium-length grasses to uncover even shorter plants, the food of the Thompson's and Grant's gazelles.

"Later those Tommies might do some sunbathing," Dick tells us. He's spent so much time around these antelopes he even knows their daily schedules. While early and late in the day are the best times for running games, between nine and ten thirty a.m. is their favorite time to catch some rays. As the other species in the mixed herd watch for predators, all the Tommies in sight may lie down. With legs folded beneath them, all face the same direction, their backs toward the warming sun.

We continue watching animals all the way across the Crater. A band of thirteen spotted hyenas, black tails bristling with excitement, is on patrol. Living in family groups dominated by females, not males, these dog-like predators fearlessly police the boundaries of their territories. If they encounter a rival group of hyenas, they'll fight. If they find lions, they'll fight. Far from being skulking scavengers, hyenas are warrior-huntresses. Even a lone hyena can take down an adult wildebeest, and lions are far more likely to steal a carcass from a hyena than the other way around. Hyenas, and not lions, are the wildebeests' most feared predator.

"'Beest alert!" calls Anna. Some distance from the patrolling hyenas, we come upon another group of wildebeests. "Ah, this is more like it!" says Dick. Though we have a long journey ahead, we can't help but stop to watch. One bull stands proud on his stamping ground, head high, immobile. "He's quite ready for action," Dick says. But alas, the nearby cows ignore him. While he stands tall, the cows graze contentedly. Some lie down, forelegs first, to chew the cud.

To our left, Logan spots a wildebeest bull taking what looks like an ordinary stroll. But Dick knows he's passing through a neighboring bull's territory. "Watch this," says Dick.

The two bulls break into a run, shaking their heads. The first bull turns, circles his neighbor, and tilts his head. It's an invitation. Dick narrates: "Are you man enough to hold this territory? Show me your testosterone!" The second bull obliges, and urinates to let the first bull analyze his chemistry. The first bull curls his front lip, exposing his vomeronasal organ. He confirms

the answer to his question is *yes*. Next, the second bull asks the same question: "What about you? Do *you* merit the land you've staked out?"

Apparently the two agree they're worthy rivals. They pause, snort—and then both whirl and drop to their knees. *Bang!* They clash horns. And then they back off, rub their heads and horns in the grass, and start grazing. The whole thing takes barely two minutes.

"If we're lucky, we'll be seeing a lot more of that, and more, very soon!" says Dick. We drive up and over the Crater's northwest rim, and begin our journey with a seventy-mile drive northwest, across the vast Serengeti plains.

The short, tan grasses are sparse and trampled, and sprinkled liberally with pellets of dung. "Looks like our friends have been through ahead of us," says Joshua.

Oh no, I think, *they've left!*

In a wide sky bruised with dark clouds, Liz notices a patch of rain falling in slanted lines. "The rain may be pulling them," says Dick.

If we can see the rain, the wildebeests can, too. But Dick has watched wildebeests react to a storm that he had learned via radio was more than fifteen miles away—rain the animals couldn't see. How do they know about it?

When the wind is right, they can surely smell it. Perhaps they sense the pungent zing of ozone, which comes when lightning splits oxygen from nitrogen. Maybe they smell the sweet, green scent known as *petrichor*—from the Greek word *petri,* for "stone," and *chor,* which roughly translates to "blood of the gods." It's created when airborne plant molecules strike minerals or clay. Or possibly the wildebeests catch the earthy whiff of wetness after the distant storm has moved off.

Yet herds will move toward rain, with its promise of fresh grass, even when the wind is carrying the scent of rain away from them. Do they listen for the rumble of thunder? How much of their route is remembered? How is it modified by their assessment of the changing conditions along the way?

We can't access the wildebeests' senses; we can't know their memories. But we can do something else: tomorrow, we plan to meet with three of Dick's colleagues in conservation biology. With the help of human technologies, they are keeping track of the wildebeest migration. Perhaps tomorrow we can get a good bead on where the big herds have gone.

Ngorongoro's Lions

AFTER A TUMULTUOUS HISTORY, THE FORTUNES OF NGORONGORO'S LIONS ARE looking up.

When Dick first moved to the Crater, lions were a rare sight. Just before he came, a flood had ushered in a plague of biting flies that so harassed the lions that they became too weak to hunt. By the time the flies left, only nine lionesses and one lion remained alive.

Over the next twelve years, their numbers rebounded, reaching 125 in 1975—becoming the densest population of lions in Africa.

But soon it was clear that something was wrong. Cubs weren't surviving. Researchers began to suspect the problem was inbreeding.

It turned out that for decades, all the lions in the Crater had been sired by the same handful of males. Normally this wouldn't happen. Lions live in resident prides, typically a couple of males, often brothers, four or five adult lionesses, and their six or seven children. Male youngsters are forced out of the pride by age three. But every few years, new males come in—usually a coalition of two or more brothers. They overthrow the old males and bring new genes to the pride.

Three lionesses at Ngorongoro Crater.

In Ngorongoro, though, new males weren't coming in. Were the Crater's walls too steep? Were herders, whose settlements ring much of the Crater, killing newcomers? Were the Ngorongoro lions' coalitions so powerful they could keep new lions out? Nobody was sure.

Then, in September 2013, a group of four mystery males, certainly brothers, showed up in the Crater. The mighty coalition of four was able to defeat the males in the largest of the Crater's four existing prides. They brought welcome new blood; they've sired some twenty cubs. Now there is even a fifth pride.

And this is good news, because elsewhere in Africa, lion populations are plummeting. The problem is people: Farms and towns encroach on land where herders once pastured their cows, goats, and sheep. The pastoralists are then pushed into ever-smaller areas. And though all that space is land that lions owned in the first place, lions can't live on farms or in towns, and when lions prey on pastoralists' livestock, the herders angrily kill the big cats for doing so.

In the past thirty years, Africa's lion population has been cut in half. They've been wiped out of West Africa entirely. If present trends continue, conservationists say that Africa's biggest cats could be gone by 2050.

Other Magnificent Migrants: Pilchard Sardines

BETWEEN MAY AND JULY, WHEN OCEAN temperatures along the coast drop below 54 degrees Fahrenheit, billions of sardines spawn in the cool waters of the Agulhas Bank and move northward along the east coast of South Africa. Shimmering shoals of migrating pilchard sardines stretch up to nine miles long and 130 feet deep along the coast. Their group is so huge they can form what looks and acts like a giant superorganism. The glittering shoals can instantly change shape, weaving through the water, the billions of small animals transforming in seconds into the appearance of one large one. Like a flock of birds expanding and contracting in flight, these masses of shoaling fish can change in an instant from a sinuous sea dragon to a monstrous living carpet to a swirling, silvery globe.

When the fish arrive to lay and fertilize their eggs off the coast of the province of KwaZulu-Natal, predators converge from miles around. Tens of thousands of black-and-white birds called Cape gannets rain from the sky. Great white, hammerhead, and ragged-tooth sharks shoot up from below. Bottlenose and common dolphins work like border collies to herd the sardines into tight "bait balls" through which they—and dozens of other predators—swim open-mouthed and gorge. Penguins, seals, tuna, marlins, and humpback whales join the hunt. And so do humans, who surge into the shallows using nets, buckets, shirts, pants, and their bare hands to catch as many of the fish as they can.

But the sardines' return migration during late winter to spring is unnoticed—at least by humans. Nobody is sure why they're not seen, but researchers guess the return route occurs at depths where the water is cooler than at the surface.

Dwarf mongooses find a termite mound that makes a good vantage point to watch for danger.

Chapter Four

Ten minutes into our first sortie the next morning, we're forced to stop. A dozen vehicles are parked on the bridge in front of us.

"Not another lion!" wails Dick.

"The only time a wildebeest gets *that* sort of attention," Anna grumbles, "is when it's being eaten."

"Lions seem to be the big thing, but it's kind of like watching your dog sleep after a big meal," says Gary.

It's true. In his *Safari Companion,* Dick noted that the typical lion spends between twenty and twenty-one hours a day resting. And in fact, the two male lions two hundred yards away from us are doing just that: lying down, doing nothing. "To see lions doing anything other than conserving energy requires luck and persistence," Dick wrote.

Yet still, notes Liz, "we look and look at them. We're fascinated. We can't take our eyes off them."

Neither can the small herd of ten zebras on the opposite side of the bridge, all facing the lions, ears tipped forward. Or the troop of olive baboons, primates like ourselves, calling with alarm from the fig trees: "WAA-hoo!"

"Like all the other species out there," says Dick, "we have a fascination with predators in our genes." Of course, it makes sense. For millennia, humans who failed to pay attention to predators got eaten by them. Even if they managed to avoid getting eaten long enough to have children, their orphans were unlikely to survive to pass on their genes.

We share a lot in common with the wildebeests and their fellow migrants. "We're all social species," Dick notes. He's right: like them, we revel in the company of our own kind. We pack into stadiums for sporting events and concerts; we crowd parade routes for public celebrations; we mass together in the streets for rallies and protests. Especially when it seems something important is happening, we're eager to be among our own kind.

We fear being alone. Like wildebeests, we, too, come from a long line of ancestors who risked being eaten by other animals. If you're one wildebeest among a herd of a million, your chance of becoming a meal for a lion is—well, one in a million. Alone, you're the only snack in sight. And to any passing predator, you'll stick out like a sore thumb when you're alone.

Only one thing is worse than being alone, says Dick: "Being *lost* and alone."

He knows. In 2007, during a safari on which he was the featured naturalist, one afternoon when the tourists were tired and wanted to nap, he wanted to keep watching animals. "I'll join you later," he told the group. He set out on foot, crossed a small stream, made a wrong turn, wandered a mile . . . and realized he was lost.

When Dick didn't return to camp, Dorobo staff searched. They built fires. They shot off guns—all to no avail. Meanwhile, dehydrating under the hot sun, Dick waited for a carpet of aggressive African bees to leave the only water source he could find—a muddy waterhole that had been excavated by elephants. He filtered the dirty water through two layers of handkerchiefs. Wearing only shorts, a T-shirt, and flip-flops, he tried to light a fire for warmth and to attract attention—but he had no matches.

Dick spent the night sitting on top of a flat portion of a twenty-foot-tall termite mound. He had only his Leatherman knife blade to protect him from lions, leopards, and hyenas.

When Dorobo staff found him in the morning, he was cold, tired, hungry. But safe. And now, he more fully understood the wildebeests' elemental, urgent need to keep up with the rest of their kind. "The wildebeests may not be taking the same paths every year," he says, "but at least they're together."

But where are they now? And will we be able to catch up with them?

⁂

"You may be just in time!"

We've arrived at Seronera, the primary control center of Serengeti National Park, where we're met by one of Dick and Anna's old friends. White-haired, pink-faced, and smoking a cigar, Swiss-born Markus Borner is the former head of the Frankfurt Zoological Society's Africa Programme, one of the great international guardians of the Serengeti. (In 1961, the society was among the first nongovernmental organizations from a developed country to help the newly independent Tanzania set up a con-

Dick with Markus Borner.

servation infrastructure to protect its wildlife—an effort many nations now support as well.) Working with the Tanzanian government, the Germany-based society has funded some of the area's most potent antipoaching forces, as well as many of its crucial animal studies.

Markus has just returned from a flight up north in a small spotter plane. He was checking on the welfare of a group of African wild dogs recently reintroduced to several areas, including inside the park. The African equivalent of the North American wolf, the Serengeti population of these handsome, tricolored dogs with large, rounded ears has been struggling to recover from a disastrous die-off from rabies and distemper, diseases they caught from domestic dogs. After Masai herders, angry with the predators, burned a wild dog den, killing the helpless puppies, the Frankfurt Zoological Society, along with the Tanzania Wildlife Research Institute, stepped in. They rescued neighboring packs and moved them to protected areas. Markus is one of the researchers who flies over the area to check on them every day. The trip affords great views of migrating wildebeest herds along the way.

And Markus believes we may be just in time to catch them.

"I think the wildebeests are really moving out right now. A great lot of them are up in the Mara already," he tells us as we sit sipping hot tea in the shade of the veranda at the Frankfurt Zoological Society's office. "Where the wild dogs are, there were long lines of gnus."

Dick nods. "We certainly hope to see them."

"The big masses," Markus says, "you'll see up north."

Based here in Seronera, over the past forty years Markus has studied subjects as varied as the social behavior of cheetahs and the travels of black rhinos. But nothing, he insists, is more crucial than understanding the complex ecology of the wildebeest migration. "Tanzania is one of the most important countries in the world from the point of view of wildlife," he reminds us, "and the migration is its dominant factor."

Ironically, even though studies like Dick's and Markus's have revealed much about the wildebeests' movements, numbers, and ecology, understanding the migration is now more, not less, complicated than ever—and far more urgent. "The problem is, it's being hemmed in by human populations," says Markus. People now affect every aspect of the wildebeests' lives, from altering rainfall patterns by changing the world's climate because of burning fossil fuels, to directly killing the animals to feed an increasing number of human mouths. And these days, poachers have a new incentive to kill wildebeests: as human populations grow, so does the appetite for meat. Even on reserves and parks where animals are legally protected, poachers consider wildebeests, hartebeests, topis, gazelles—even giraffes and monkeys—as sources of free protein. It's called "bushmeat."

"Where are the poachers coming from these days?" Dick asks.

A male olive baboon with infant.

"The poachers are coming mainly from the western Serengeti," reports Markus.

And the carnage? "They poach a hundred thousand wildebeests a year."

I'm stunned. How long can this go on, before all the wildebeests are killed?

"It's quite interesting," answers Markus. "The population can sustain it—for now."

What? "It's mainly the young males getting snared," he says. These bachelors typically start out in the lead of the migration. While the territorial bulls stake out their real estate, the bachelor males seek the shady areas at the edges of the migrants' path, horning trees to get out their aggression—and this is where poachers set their snares. "That's maybe why the population can sustain it," Markus suggests, "for now. But," he adds ominously, "Africa's population will dou-ble in the next twenty years."

Will human appetites literally eat the greatest migration on earth into oblivion? Or will our numbers simply crowd the biggest mass of mammals off the face of the planet? It's a sickening possibility—but it's happened before.

"The moving multitude . . . darkened the whole plain," wrote explorers Meriwether Lewis and William Clark about the seemingly endless migratory bison herds they saw in South Dakota in 1806. There may have been thirty to seventy-five million of them. There were only twenty-eight wild plains buffaloes left by the turn of the century. Only a few hundred thousand survive today, and their great migration is a thing of the past.

We need cheering up, so Markus bids us goodbye with an encouraging suggestion: we could phone Frankfurt's Serengeti Conservation Project director, Mark Jenkins, in the morning. He'll be flying on antipoaching patrols along the migration route every day. His report might be a helpful supplement to the intel we're about to gather at our next stop—perhaps the most detailed and up-to-date data we'll be able to get about the migration.

For Dick and Anna, it's a homecoming: The simple cinder-block structure with its poured concrete floors and corrugated tin roof today houses cheetah researchers. But from 1978 to 1981, it was the Esteses' home. Here, Anna acquired the scars she still has on her knees from scrambling over the piles of ancient metamorphic rock boulders called kopjes ("COP-ees")—it means "small head" in the Afrikaans language—with her brother. Here, she spent hours playing hide-and-seek with weasel-ish mongooses and little woodchuck-like hyraxes. From the porch, Dick and Runi used to watch the storms roll over the plains. And it's here that we've come to meet with two of Dick's fellow wildebeest experts, young researchers from University of Glasgow in Scotland.

While the others continue on a game drive, Dick, Anna, Gary, and I sit down on the porch with Grant Hopcraft and about a dozen small wild lizards on the patio. Blond and bespectacled, Grant leads a team from the Scottish university that has equipped twenty-five wildebeests and fifteen zebras with high-tech GPS collars. As they move, the collars beam each animal's location to orbiting satellites, which then transmit their data right to the researchers' mobile phones.

"That's a change!" laughs Dick. When he first used wildlife tracking collars in the 1970s, they were new, bulky, and unreliable. The devices used very high frequency (VHF) radio waves—the kind used for walkie-talkies. You could only pick up the signal if you were closely following the animal on foot, in a vehicle, or on a plane. At best, they lasted eight weeks before the batteries died. "Now," said Grant, "we sit here and we're swamped by text messages from our wildebeests!" And the trim, half-pound GPS collars last two or three years.

The data coming in from Grant's forty animals suggests that while the wildebeests in the Crater haven't rutted, the Serengeti rut may be

Dick with researchers Grant Hopcraft (right) and Tom Morrison (left).

early. One of his collared animals is way ahead of schedule. "We had one female wildebeest, number 5028, who went straight to the Mara and arrived a week ago! No stopping!" Masai Mara is the northern extension of the Serengeti into Kenya—and usually the great migration wouldn't be expected to arrive there for another couple of weeks.

Why was she in such a rush? What would be the benefit of getting to the Mara before the others? Dick suggests one reason: "She could be the first to get the greenest, freshest grasses on the north side of the Mara."

"But the journey is arduous," notes Grant. He wonders if that female's calf from last year was strong enough to travel that far that fast.

We're thrilled to learn we can follow Grant's wildebeests and zebras too. We write down the website: www.serengeti-tracker.org. We can find his collared animals by clicking on Serengeti Map. (You can, too!) Grant checks his phone and reports that most of his collared animals right now are nearing a place called Nyasarori— a ranger post between Serengeti National Park and the Grumeti Reserves. And that's great, because we are heading through the park to Grumeti in a few days. We hope we can catch up.

But Grant notes two caveats for us to consider. When we check the website, we should keep in mind that the site doesn't differentiate between the zebras and the wildebeests (today, if you check the website, the icons for the two animals are different), and sometimes the two species part company. More important, he points out, "We've got collars on forty animals. So what? That's a drop in the bucket." There's no telling whether these forty individuals are with the big herds.

"We're trying to get the next round of collaring started soon," he says. In November, his team will be outfitting even more animals with satellite collars, including wildebeests in populations that do not migrate. "It's going to be interesting seeing what's going on with the resident animals," he says.

It will be particularly interesting to compare this data with that amassed by Grant's colleague, who has just arrived from the field. Tom Morrison, tall and dark-haired, has studied a different subspecies of wildebeest, the eastern white-bearded gnu, in Tarangire National Park.

Located to the south of Ngorongoro, encompassing 1,100 square miles, Tarangire is dwarfed by Serengeti National Park's 5,700 square miles. Of course, Tarangire's gnu population has always been smaller. But it was a substantial population of forty-five thousand with an ecologically important, 150-mile migration of its own, taking the animals from their dry-season range in the park to their wet-season range north, outside of the park's protected boundary.

That is, the population *was* substantial—until recently. During a period of less than fifteen years, the eastern white-bearded gnu population crashed. Government programs encouraged farming in the animals' wet-season range. Hunters were allowed to "cull" gnus unrestricted. "All kinds of people were just killing animals willy-nilly. Actual, professional hunters were in tears" over the carnage, Tom said.

But by the time the government reversed its policies, it was too late. By the turn of the millennium, the eastern white-bearded gnu numbers had plummeted to three thousand. Less than a tenth of them remained.

"I'm sure this caused a huge change in the ecosystem," Tom tells us, and "of course, the migration was disrupted."

Historically, the Tarangire gnus, along with thousands of other antelopes and zebras, migrated along ten different north-to-south, south-to-north routes. Now most of those routes are blocked by human settlements. Today only two of the traditional migratory routes are thought to remain. And they are radically shifting. Tom's studies confirmed a widespread belief that the routes were moving east; he also discovered another significant change that no one else suspected. "I've found them 120 kilo-

Though zebras and wildebeests often travel together, sometimes the two part ways.

meters [75 miles] north of the expected route!" Tom tells us.

Can a change that dramatic still provide the animals with what they need to survive? Which wildebeests are making the decision to shift? What's driving their decision? What's the impact of this change on the area's other animals? On its grasses, trees, soil?

"We know from your studies here that wildebeests play a huge role," Tom tells Dick. "But unlike in Serengeti, there's not been a lot of research in Tarangire. We know only roughly what the herbivores have been doing over time. My project investigated where the wildebeests were migrating—and what are the consequences of the change."

As Africa's wild places shrink, the natural movements of all wild animals is an increasingly endangered phenomenon. The animals are hemmed in by humans on all sides. Fences block them. Roads bisect their range. Farmers steal their habitat. Domestic animals threaten them with contagious disease. Poachers shoot and snare them.

"This is the story of all the migratory systems in Africa," Dick tells us dejectedly. Except for in the Serengeti ecosystem, all the really large populations of wildebeests have crashed. Only two of the remaining populations—that in Tarangire, and one in the country of Zambia, to Tanzania's southwest—now continue their magnificent migrations.

"Here in Serengeti, this is the last great migration that hasn't been disrupted," Dick tells us as we say goodbye to our new friends. Before the 1900s, there were dozens of wildebeest migrations in Africa. "This is the last one we've been able to save." He pauses, thinking of the bushmeat trade, global climate change, East Africa's exponential human population growth . . . "Up to now," he adds.

As we travel on to our new camp, in Serengeti National Park, that afternoon, my heart sinks. The spectacle of the great migration may not be here to see forever.

This could be our last chance.

The Cost of a Migration Disrupted

IT MAKES SENSE THAT WHEN THE WILDEBEESTS' ANCIENT TREK IS DISRUPTED, the species who migrate with them—like zebras, Tommies, and elands—would suffer too. But what about species that don't even join the throng? Could they be affected as well?

A study in Tarangire National Park by a team from the United States and Europe found that the disruption to the wildebeest migration there could have wide-ranging effects. Among the collateral casualties may be the world's tallest living land animal, the long-lashed, spotted "tall blonde" who we count among the most charismatic and beloved creatures in Africa: the giraffe.

Giraffes don't migrate—but they benefit from the wildebeests' journey just the same. When the trekking wildebeests come sweeping through Tarangire, they share the savanna with giraffes, many of whom are taking care of young babies. After a rather startling birth (dropping head-and-front-legs-first six feet to the ground!), giraffe calves can't stand up for thirty minutes; and even once they've gained their feet, they tire easily. Their stride is so much shorter than their parents' that they can't possibly keep up. So new giraffe moms often hide their infants in the grass while they forage. When the calves are several weeks old, the moms leave the babies in a sort of kindergarten group of up to nine youngsters. Even though the group is overseen by an adult female babysitter, the baby giraffes are easy prey for predators. More than half of all giraffe babies are eaten before they're a month old.

That's one reason the flood of migrating wildebeests is so welcome in Tarangire. The presence of so many wildebeests gives the local lions something to eat other than baby giraffes. The study found that the presence of so many wildebeests had "significant [positive] effects on giraffe population dynamics." The more wildebeests there are, the more giraffe calves survive.

But "If wildebeest populations continue to decline," wrote the lead author of the study, Dr. Derek Lee of the Wild Nature Institute, "then giraffe populations will also be negatively impacted." And giraffes can't afford to take that hit. In the last three decades, their population has declined by 40 percent. Because of poaching and human encroachment, fewer than one hundred thousand of the nine different kinds of giraffe still survive on the entire African continent.

Scientists are only now starting to understand the scope of the migration's impact. But one thing is already clear: severing the wildebeests' remaining migratory routes would be "catastrophic," says Tom.

Giraffes benefit from the wildebeest migration, too.

Other Magnificent Migrants: Christmas Island Red Crabs

THE TRIP IS ONLY FIVE MILES LONG. BUT THE SIGHT OF FORTY MILLION BIG, bright-red crabs with claws four inches long clattering out of the forest, flooding across roads, and plunging into the sea is so impressive that the migration is a major tourist attraction at their island home off Australia's Indian Ocean coast.

For most of the year, the red crabs live unseen in burrows they dig in the rainforest. Triggered by the onset of the rainy season and the phases of the moon, the crabs leave their burrows and begin the weeklong journey to the coast to spawn. The male

crabs usually arrive a few days before the females. While they await the ladies, they dig new "welcoming" burrows—their honeymoon suites. After mating, males crawl back to the forest, but the females remain. Inside the burrows, they incubate their eggs, and wait. Then, precisely at the turn of high tide during the last quarter of the moon, they rush to the sea and, raising their claws toward the night sky, shake their eggs from the undersides of their bodies in what looks like a shimmying, ecstatic dance. In the days that follow, the females return to their shady homes in the rainforest.

The babies hatch immediately. Many of them will feed whales and sharks and fish; spectacular whale sharks time their visits to Christmas Island to coincide with the crabs' spawning. But those lucky larvae who survive will, within days, return to land, shed their exoskeletons, and transform themselves into air breathers. The tiny crabs will make their way to the forest like their parents. In five years, they'll grow big enough to take part in the migration to spawn themselves.

In recent years, millions of crabs have been killed by accidentally imported "crazy ants." But so beloved are the pretty red crustaceans (and so financially valuable are the tourists who flock to see their annual trek) that Australians have taken action to help them. They can't seem to eradicate the ants, but the locals can protect the crabs from another scourge: cars. Some roads are closed during the migration, barriers have been erected along many streets, and a bridge and several tunnels have been constructed to help ensure for the crabs a safer journey to the sea.

The Other Serengeti

THE FAMOUS NATURALIST JOHN JAMES AUDUBON HAD SPENT ALMOST HIS whole life exploring America's wildest and most beautiful places, painting its animals. But in the summer of 1843, as he traveled up the Missouri River to the heart of the American Great Plains, he was unprepared for the sights that greeted him.

Enormous herds of bison grazed the prairie with their calves; elk forded the river. Bighorn sheep gazed at him from the summit of a hill, while a wolf lay down like a dog on a sandbar. Grizzlies were so common he could often see three at a glance.

At the end of one incredible day, the great artist was still stunned as he sat down to write to his wife.

"In fact, it is *impossible to describe or even conceive* the vast multitudes of these animals that exist even now, and feed on these ocean-like prairies," he wrote in his letter.

The amazing assortment of animals—especially the numberless herds of bison who flowed by like a roiling, living river—"was one of the great spectacles of the world," wrote naturalist Dan Flores about the last big animals on the Great Plains. Two centuries ago, the prairie ecosystem in the middle of our country was so like the African savanna that Flores titled his book *American Serengeti*.

In fact, the grasslands covering ten of our western states once teemed with animal abundance that dwarfs today's Serengeti. Researchers say that the magnificent American bison (also called buffaloes) were once the most numerous large mammals ever to roam our planet. They dominated the landscape from the Missouri River to the Rocky Mountains, from Mexico to Saskatchewan. They traveled in numbers so large that in 1871, a soldier wrote home that it took him *six days* to ride through a single herd. The sound they made when traveling earned them the name "The Thunder of the Plains." And the buffaloes, like the wildebeests, created and maintained an ecosystem that sustained scores of other animal species, as well as people.

Native Americans across this vast swath of prairie depended on the buffaloes. Each slain animal provided for food (some people enjoyed eating even the nose gristle, raw, for a treat), clothing (even the sinew was used for sewing), housing (tepees were made from the hides), warmth (folks burned the dung for fuel), and utensils (carved from hooves and horns). The bison provided spiritual sustenance, too. The Plains Indians understood that the buffaloes had families and memories, and thought that if human souls survived after death, buffalo souls did, too.

But the white hunters arriving in ever-increasing numbers after Audubon's visit saw buffaloes differently. Having already killed almost all the beavers from the Midwest for their pelts by midcentury, white trappers descended on the Plains buffaloes and began slaughtering them for their hides and tongues. They killed some three hundred thousand annually. The transcontinental railroad, completed in 1869, accelerated the carnage. Massive hunting parties arrived to kill the animals just for sport. One hunter boasted he had personally killed six thousand buffaloes by himself. People shot buffaloes from moving trains and often left the carcasses to rot.

By 1884, only 325 bison were left—25 of them in Yellowstone National Park. But legal, commercial shipment of hides continued until it was finally outlawed in 1889!

By then, ranchers and their cattle had usurped the land of the Native Americans and buffaloes. But unlike the buffaloes, cattle did not evolve here. They died in the

American bison were once the most numerous large animals on earth.

summer heat and winter snowstorms. The settlers next tried planting wheat on the plains, but it wasn't as hardy as the native buffalo grass. Drought killed the new crops. And with no plant roots to anchor the soil to the ground, in the 1930s, winds brought horrific dust storms that blocked the sun for weeks on end and persisted for years. "Raging, grit-filled winds shattered windows and scoured the paint off houses and cars," wrote Don Brown in *The Great American Dust Bowl*. Plagues of ants, centipedes, and black widow spiders infested homes because birds and bats that would normally kill and eat them had died. The "black blizzard" even blew Midwestern dirt all the way to Boston and New York, where the sight of the Statue of Liberty was obscured by a freakish gray haze of dust. The almost complete eradication of the native buffaloes ignited an environmental catastrophe that devastated the continent for a decade. Some say the states known then as the Dust Bowl never completely recovered.

In 1905, a handful of private citizens stepped in to try to save the buffaloes from complete extinction. The American Bison Society was formed by supporters of the New York Zoological Society, now the Bronx Zoo. By capturing some of the last remaining wild bison and breeding them in captivity, they were able to restore buffaloes to sufficient numbers that some could again be set free. Thanks to the restoration program, today about twenty-five thousand bison roam wild on public lands, and another five hundred thousand now live on private preserves, including Native American lands. Some are bred like cattle for eventual slaughter; others are hunted respectfully in the Native American tradition; some are not hunted at all.

Though the conservationists managed to save the buffaloes from disappearing, the spectacle of the thundering herd animals is extinct. And even though the killing happened more than a century ago, to historians who look back upon it, the sheer scale of the destruction is as stunning today as was the sight of all those wild beasts back in Audubon's day.

"This single American region experienced the largest wholesale destruction of animal life discoverable in modern history," wrote Flores. To him, the blame, and the lesson, is clear: "We stood by, and allowed what happened to the great plains a century ago, the destruction of one of the ecological wonders of the world . . . a myopic, chaotic, unthinking destruction, and, I think, immoral."

Chapter Five

Our quarters at Pembezoni Camp are spectacular. Our tall canvas tents are set directly on the plain of Serengeti National Park. Wild animals can literally come to our doorstep. That's why guards armed with spears escort us from our dining tent to our sleeping tents—to protect us from lions and leopards, hyenas and hippos. The only downside of our splendid isolation is that we're having trouble getting an internet connection to check up on Grant's collared wildebeests.

We hope to be able to get internet reception tomorrow night at our next camp. Later this afternoon, Anna will try to phone Markus's Frankfurt Zoological Society colleague, Mark Jenkins, to see whether he spotted wildebeest armies on his morning's aerial surveys. In the meantime, we decide to go out on an early-morning game drive, to see what we might find.

During a pause in the safari, Logan practices his balancing act on a makeshift tightrope constructed from a tow rope at our camp.

Soon enough, someone finds *us:* a solitary elephant. Though elephants sometimes ignore vehicles, at other times, they approach, curious. Occasionally the pachyderms chase cars, trumpeting, ears flapping—in which case, it's best to get out of the twelve-thousand-pound animal's way.

This one seems only briefly interested in us, but we're enthralled. As he turns away, we're all snapping photos of his ample, wrinkly rear end. But Dick has his eyes on something else.

"A crèche of baby impalas!"

Though wildebeests are his favorites, Dick considers impalas "the perfect antelope": brown and white, about the size of a Grant's gazelle, the impala is known for its spectacular, playful leaps,

up to three yards high and eleven yards long. Sometimes several impalas leap at the same time, often landing on the forelegs while executing an almost vertical kick of the hind legs.

The seven babies in this crèche, guarded by two adult females, are rapidly nibbling leaves from the tips of short bushes now. "Let's count the males and females," suggests Dick. With impalas, it's easy: only the males have horns, which appear within two months of birth.

Eventually those horns will grow into marvelous, S-curved, ridged headgear that can reach three feet long. But in another two months, the three males we count will find their growing horns becoming a big problem, Dick explains. They'll attract the attention of adult male impa-

An impala can leap ten feet—over vegetation or even over other impalas.

las, who will chase and harass the young males out of the herd. By the time their horns are as long as their ears, they'll be forced to leave the safety of the experienced adults and join a bachelor group with other young males. It's a risky time.

Horns are one of the defining features of antelopes, Dick explains. These marvelous structures—they're made of keratin, as are fingernails and hair, but coating a bony core—have many uses other than weaponry. While it's true that horns are tremendously effective tools for fighting, the structures may be even more important in advertising—including false advertising!

Horns are a badge of maleness, and size matters. Sometimes all a male has to do is advertise his horns by shaking his head—"Watch out! My horns are bigger than yours!"—to get a rival to back away. Sometimes he has to resort to actual combat to defend his territory or his females.

But in forty-three African species, including the wildebeest, *females* also have horns.

Why? Biologists have wondered for decades. The conventional view is that females use them for self-defense. True, Dick has seen females use their horns to defend themselves and their babies. But his careful studies show that females without horns seem to enjoy about equal success in protecting their young as females who do have them.

Dick has a different idea. Perhaps, he theorizes, females evolved horns for something even more important: to delay the ejection of their male offspring from the protection of the herd. If everyone has horns, the dominant male can't figure out who to kick out—at least not till the young are old enough to fend for themselves.

Sound far-fetched? "Consider that male mimicry isn't limited to horns," says Dick. This was abundantly clear in 1999 when he and Roger were, in Roger's words, "roaming across the Serengeti, aging and sexing." As part of Dick's study, the two of them were surveying the wildebeest herds, trying to estimate the animals' ages (a lucky wildebeest can live up to twenty years in the wild; longer in a zoo) and sort males from females. The work wasn't easy. Besides horns, females even have a tuft on the belly exactly where you'd expect to find male equipment. Females also sport beards, manes, and coloration virtually identical to those of males. It takes a practiced eye, and good binoculars, to tell the sexes apart.

And if that weren't evidence enough for Dick's theory, there's also this: the species in which the males and females look most alike are also the species that most benefit from keeping the young males in the herd. The beautiful, nomadic gazelles called oryxes, with lance-like, ridged horns, inhabit harsh, unpredictable deserts; if young males were kicked out of the herd, they might never find any other oryxes for company in the vast, empty spaces. "The horns of the oryx are so important, they appear *in utero,*" says Dick. Yes—they actually start growing horns in their mother's womb! Anna and I shoot each other a grimace, imagining the

discomfort of the mother. "The horns come out flat against the head and then stand up," Dick assures us.

"As long as males and females look alike, competition between males is minimal," he continues. Reducing competition—and aggression—is particularly important in gregarious and migratory species like wildebeests. Impalas, in contrast, don't migrate, and their herds seldom exceed one hundred. They frequently number mere dozens.

So in wildebeests, while horns are about combat, they're also about keeping the peace. Togetherness is crucial to species like the wilde-

As with wildebeests, both male and female oryxes sport horns.

beest. And just around the corner, we'd be visiting a species for which togetherness is taken to an extreme.

⁕⁕⁕

As the heat of noon approaches, Joshua takes us to the pool—but not one we'd like to swim in! Here, hippos seem as tightly packed as cobblestones. Even though there's plenty of space in the muddy water, more than a hundred hippos are jammed into an area smaller than a backyard patio. At night, when it's cool, they'll emerge to graze, and won't tolerate such close quarters. But for now, this is the only way everyone can stand on the bottom of the pool and still enjoy the buoyant embrace of the water. Heavy jaws rest on each others' fat backsides and shoulders, using each other as living pillows. "But they can get even more packed than this!" says Joshua—literally cheek by jowl. I can't imagine it.

Occasionally the head of a little baby hippo pokes up in a space between the rounded bodies. The hippos use their tails to constantly flip

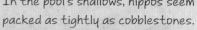
In the pool's shallows, hippos seem packed as tightly as cobblestones.

the soupy, brownish-green water onto their own backs to stay cool and help protect their thin, delicate skin from sunburn. (They also have glands beneath the skin that produce a red fluid, which looks alarming, but functions as a natural sunscreen.) Occasionally a new hippo arrives from on land and crashes the party, and then everyone rearranges themselves noisily, grousing and gaping. But most of the time, they seem as contented as Florida sunbathers on a beach.

What a relief to these huge animals to be able to give their one-ton bulk to the water to hold them. And I suspect this is why they complain so loudly when jostled: they are luxuriating in comfort—a state so perfect that even a tiny change is upsetting. Is this sense of cozy contentment what the wildebeests feel when, during a pause in the migration, they can rest in the company of hundreds of thousands of their own kind? Perhaps togetherness like this offers them their most perfect peace: I imagine they feel supported when surrounded by a sea of fellow wildebeests, as far as their eyes can see.

In the afternoon, we head out to explore a different habitat: the kopjes at the edge of Seronera, the central region of the park.

Off to our left we see them: the rocks are narrow and tall, like a long row of jagged skyscrapers. Trees of different species—thorny acacias, cactus-like euphorbia with yellow flowers—jut out of the boulders at odd angles. A fig tree pours its roots over the rocks like a frozen waterfall. The kopjes stretch for a quarter mile.

Kopjes, composed of some of the oldest rocks on the planet, provide a habitat for animals from lizards to mammals.

Agama lizard.

Like its relative, the elephant, the hyrax sports tusks, albeit small ones. The gland on the back secretes fluid used in communication.

These rocks (some of the oldest on the planet, dating to five hundred million years ago) provide a completely different habitat from the surrounding grasslands and woods, Dick explains. Kopjes provide a refuge from grass fires. They offer a vantage point for predators. They contain many cracks and crannies—and these are the homes of the little hyraxes: the agile, guinea-pig-like animals who numbered among Anna's favorite childhood playmates.

"Here the bush and the rock hyrax live together," says Dick. Even though they are two different species, they cohabitate in harmony. With binoculars, we can see about a dozen—but there may be fifty or more. They're standing and sitting on little ledges, like people in rockers on their front porches. From crevices in the stones we see white markings that have dripped down. These are urine marks from a common latrine, the group showing others of their kind that this stony refuge is taken.

But daily, the rock hyraxes must leave the safety of their stony lairs. While the bush hyraxes eat the leaves of acacia trees and other plants, the rock hyraxes must venture from their sanctuary to graze. Led by an experienced adult, and usually guarded by the dominant male, a party of hyraxes descends to pastures up to a hundred yards away in the mornings and afternoons. If the male spots a predator, he gives a loud squeak—one of twenty-one different calls that some researchers now think might function like words in human language. The alarm call sends everyone scurrying back to the safety of the cracks in the kopje.

If they can make it.

"Think what it takes for them to leave these rocks and venture onto the plain!" Dick says. He invites us to imagine their bravery and desperation as these five-pound animals cross open territory, filled with predators large and small. These are the most raptor-filled skies I've ever seen—we witness dozens of birds of prey each day. Much of the time, the birds are looking for

hyraxes. Eagles are probably their most dangerous predator, says Dick. "But then, everyone eats hyraxes," Joshua observes—from lions to jackals to cobras. Even mongooses will take the babies.

Yet the courageous little hyrax seems to have the heart of an elephant—to which it is, surprisingly, closely related. Elephants, hyraxes, and sea cows (which include the gentle manatees beloved in Florida) comprise their own group within the mammals. They are as closely related to each other as bears are to dogs and seals. Though they don't look a bit alike on the outside—one huge and naked, one small and furry, and the third aquatic—you can see the

similarity when they open their mouths. They share ridged molars and premolars, creating a washboard surface to crush the tough vegetation they're specialized to eat. And like elephants, sea cows and hyraxes sport upper tusks (although their tusks are much smaller). Baby hyraxes nurse from nipples on the mother's chest, as elephants and sea cows do—not from an udder near the back legs as with wildebeests.

Occasionally, hyraxes must undertake a journey even longer and more perilous than they do for grazing. Adolescent males are forced out of the colony at the tender age of two. To find a new refuge means finding a new kopje—which

The mother cheetah rushes after the Tommy, but returns, unsuccessful, to her three waiting cubs.

A termite mound makes a great perch for a cheetah scanning the plains for prey.

might be a mile or more away. If they run out of food, for instance, the entire colony must relocate. This, says Dick, is a migration of sorts. Imagining these little rodent-like animals undertaking a journey of miles, under raptor-filled skies, through territory laced with huge land predators, gives me new appreciation for the perils our wildebeest armies undertake every day on their migration.

The tassels of the grasses are glowing pale amber in the golden late afternoon light when Dick notices a male bull Tommy to our left. "He's an adult, on territory. Very alert," he says. He wonders what the antelope is looking at. Ahead, about eighty yards away, we see

three safari vehicles stopped by the side of the road. They are all looking at the same thing. We follow their gaze to see, seated in the pale grass, an adult cheetah.

Binoculars rise to faces. Logan and Roger hoist their cameras. Now we see that in addition to the big cheetah, there are also three yearling cubs. Their mother, ears forward, looks intently at the Tommy, her eyes blazing orange. She stands. Muscles flow into position. She gathers her legs beneath her, coiled like a spring—and she's off, a straight-out run!

The speediest animal on earth, a cheetah can go from zero to forty miles per hour in three huge strides—each of which can carry the cat twenty-five feet. Her spine curves up and down as her legs bunch and extend. As she runs, her hind legs stretch forward almost past her ears. She can reach a speed of seventy miles per hour, as fast as a car on a highway. The Thompson's is slower, but he has a strategy. He zigzags. While running, a cheetah may take up to 150 breaths per minute, and she can run only four hundred to six hundred yards before dangerously over-heating. She comes within twenty yards of the Tommy before she realizes she can't catch him. With the slouching grace of a basketball player, she slinks back to her original place with her cubs and lies down in the molten afternoon light.

"Wow," says Liz.

"That was fantastic!" says Roger.

"I think I got the shot," says Logan.

Our hearts are still pounding from having witnessed such a show of speed and power. We can't help but feel a little disappointed for the cheetah mother and her cubs.

Except for Dick. What is his takeaway from this incandescent encounter with the fastest mammal on earth?

"That," says Dick, "shows you the exposure you face as a territorial male wildebeest."

Though we've only spotted a handful of wildebeests all day—a few territorial males, each alone on the plain—they've never been far from our thoughts. All the species we've been lucky enough to see today have, thanks to Dick, shown us something important about wildebeests—the animal who has sculpted the habitat that all these other animals share.

Our wildebeest safari is also teaching us to look deeper. We're not just learning to spot animals we would have missed. We're starting to see how these animals of the Serengeti live, and what their behavior reveals about their private lives. Sometimes, as Dick shows us, with subtle movements, an animal can unveil its most intimate secrets. But first you need to learn how to see them.

⎯⎯⎯⎯⎯⎯

Because they hide in thickets or rest near tree trunks, dik-diks—tiny antelopes named for their loud, breathy alarm call, which sounds like *zik-zik*—are hard to spot. But of course Dick spots them, and we're treated to a sighting of

what at seems, at first glance, like two pocket-size deer. Standing less than two feet tall, dik-diks weigh only about five pounds. They're the world's second-smallest antelopes—only the royal antelope, at eight inches tall, is smaller.

"Let's watch," says Dick. "The fact that they're so close together increases the chance they'll do something interesting."

With long back legs flexed, the two dik-diks mince forward on hooves so tiny each could stand on a dime. The first animal freezes, one front leg raised midstep. "They're on alert!" Dick whispers. The first one, whose spike horns show him to be a male, moves his head cautiously; his mate remains still except for the quivering tip of her long nose. They decide we pose no danger.

What happens next is something that few people would notice—and if they did, they'd find it unremarkable. The female steps ahead. She squats, urinates, then drops some little pellets of dung. The male, behind her, paws the spot, then leaves his own mark. They walk on.

Anna, observing the female through binoculars, notes she spotted a trace of blood when the female peed.

"I thought so," Dick whispers. "So she has a fawn. She may have given birth last night or this morning."

Somewhere very near, their hours-old newborn is hiding. The parents, who mate for life, must be especially adamant now about staking their territory. Next the male approaches a twig and appears to purposely poke himself in the eye. "That always looks terrible!" says Anna. But she knows what the dik-diks are doing: they are leaving a tarry secretion from a gland in front of

73

the inner corner of the eye on the stalk, further evidence that this land is theirs.

These behaviors are known in field biology as ceremonies. For the animals involved, they are just as important as the ceremonies we humans celebrate: graduation ceremonies, wedding ceremonies, communion ceremonies. By marking their territory together in this special ritual, the dik-diks reaffirm their pair bond, and make clear their claim to their land. They are committing themselves with extra vigor to their home and to each other, now that they have a fawn. They must be extra vigilant, lest other dik-diks encroach on their leafy refuge. They are saying: "This is OUR land! OUR home! It's sacred and untouchable! Strangers, keep out!"

Very few people, even researchers, ever see a newborn dik-dik. Not even the parents see them much. One study, which Dick cites in his field guide, found that a dik-dik mom spends less than one hour in twenty-four with her infant, so careful is she to keep her baby a secret.

Learning of the fawn's presence was perhaps even more special because we didn't actually see it. We didn't have to. By reading the parent dik-diks' behavior, Dick revealed to us a precious, living treasure that nobody else would guess was even there. "We just saw something very exciting," Dick says softly. "We were lucky to witness it."

Our spectacular day is capped at dinner with good news. Anna managed to reach Markus's friend, Mark Jenkins, after his afternoon antipoaching flyover. He reported seeing great numbers of migrating wildebeests massing near Nyasarori, just twenty-two miles away from our next campsite.

"So we could see masses of wildebeests tomorrow?" Gary asks hopefully.

"They were there at four p.m. today," says Joshua. "That doesn't mean they'll be there tomorrow, though."

"It's always good to keep expectations under control," cautions Anna, "because the wildebeests can disappear overnight."

"You never really know," agrees Joshua. "But that's the thrill of it. Every day can be different from the day before. Every year can be different from the year before. There are no reruns on safari!"

Other Magnificent Migrants: Loggerhead Sea Turtles

IMMEDIATELY UPON HATCHING, THEY SCRAMBLE TO THE SEA. THUS BEGINS EV-ery two-inch hatchling loggerhead sea turtle's epic, solo, eight-thousand-mile journey. Each turtle swims from the southeastern U.S. coast into the North Atlantic subtropical gyre—the circular current system that flows around the Sargasso Sea. Each female makes a single circuit of the Atlantic Ocean before returning to the beach where she was born—a migration that may take six to fifteen years.

All sea turtles migrate. But no migration is longer, more spectacular, or more fraught with danger than the loggerhead's.

These babies face a migration that might take fifteen years to complete

Like most hatchling turtles, loggerheads hatch en masse, but travel alone. None have made the trip before. They can swim only about half a mile an hour. They're too light to dive. That's why only about one in four thousand of the loggerheads hatched on Florida's beaches survives long enough to breed. How do *any* survive?

According to a team of University of North Carolina marine biologists, loggerheads—and possibly many other animals—are born with an inherited "magnetic map" that tells them where to go. In fact, turtles obtain much more complex spatial representations from magnetic fields than people obtain from their compasses, the researchers insist. This precise information allows them to "swim smart" and choose the least dangerous possible route on a journey that is packed with perils.

They must dodge the jaws of predators. They also must avoid frigid waters, where they could freeze to death. They must conserve energy. They must steer clear of forceful currents that would sweep them away from their path.

The young loggerheads respond to a particular magnetic field near northern Portugal by turning south. This response helps them stay in warm waters and avoid being swept north into cold waters near Great Britain and Scandinavia. Other magnetic information helps them stay in deep water, where predators are fewer than in the shallows.

Adaptations like these have helped loggerheads successfully complete one of the most arduous migrations on earth for hundreds of millions of years. But none of this prepared them for the threats posed by the exploding population of humans. People eat turtles and their eggs by the ton. We tangle them in our fishing nets and catch them on our hooks. We poison them with pollution; we choke them on plastic garbage tossed into the sea. Human-caused climate disruption may be altering the ocean's currents. Artificial lights confuse hatchlings trying to follow the moon to the water. Hotels, condos, and ATVs destroy nesting beaches. Because of people, after millions of years of successfully dodging myriad natural dangers, every species of sea turtle on earth is now threatened or endangered.

Evidence of the throng that has just passed is everywhere.

Chapter Six

Finally, we're on their trail.

Just an hour after we leave Pembezoni Camp for Mbalageti, evidence of passing wildebeest armies is everywhere. "You can tell some big herds have been through here," Dick says. "The grass is really chopped." The earth is trampled, the ground nearly bare.

We're driving along the Mbalageti River, a place Dick knows well. Here, in the Western Corridor of Serengeti National Park, he followed radio-collared wildebeests from 1978 to 1980 and in 1995 and 2000—yielding data that showed, for the first time, that the route and pace of the migration was far more variable than previously thought.

The migration does not consist solely of one giant herd mindlessly following one prescribed

Neighboring bull wildebeests dispute their territorial boundaries.

route year after year. Dick's studies showed that the gnus traveled not in one great mass, but in huge but separate armies, sometimes in the hundreds of thousands; and that while some armies took one route, often another group would take a different one. There's more to their travels than following the rains and green grasses.

What guides their choices? It's far more varied and sophisticated than first expected. Dick's maps of the wildebeests' movements, when compared with others by scientists studying soils and grasslands, showed that the gnus' migration may be tracking grasses so they arrive when the plants offer the wildebeests the best nutrition. And this not only varies from place to place; it changes with the seasons. Yet somehow, the wildebeests time their migration to arrive on pastures at the very moment that the grasses offer precisely that.

"And they give back what they eat," Dick tells us. The migrating wildebeests, with their droppings and urine, provide the grasses with

their main sources of essential fertilizers, nitrogen and ammonia. "No mechanical manure spreader could cover the ground more efficiently," Dick observes. "And the trampling of their hooves is like plowing a field. Grasslands actually degrade when a migration doesn't come through!"

Unlike livestock, the wildebeests and their associates don't stay in an area month after month. The grass regenerates. There's no erosion. That's all because the wildebeests move on.

Surely, we think, they must be just ahead of us.

———————

We reach the Nyasarori Bridge, where eight full-grown crocs, including a very round fellow who may weigh more than a thousand pounds, lounge along the shallows of one bank; thirty hippos mass on the other. Is an unlucky wildebeest what gives that croc his round tummy?

A line of yellow-billed storks stands watching the crocs and hippos from shore. Swifts with orange rumps and forked black tails swirl, gleaning insects, in the foreground on the opposite side of the bridge. These birds, too, are evidence of the passing parade: bugs stirred up by the wildebeests' churning hooves provide a feast for them.

Unfortunately for us, the birds can't eat all the bugs—and *we* are providing a feast for some of *them*. Our car is buzzing with tsetse flies—impressively large insects with tightly folded wings, who look like a cross between a housefly and a bee. "The tsetse flies are making music for us," says Joshua cheerfully.

And soon the flies elicit percussion and lyrics as well. *ZZzzz-zzz . . . SLAP! ZZzzzzz . . . Ack! ZZZzzz . . . Ow!* They fly inside our shirts and bite; they crawl up our pants and bite; and when they do, it hurts! By the time we feel the bite and hit them, they're full of our blood, which splatters everywhere. But we soon discover that unless we completely flatten them with our strike, they zombie-resurrect to fly up and bite us again.

The tsetses seem to especially like the back of the Land Cruiser, where Logan and Roger are wearing shorts. By noon, Logan, with an acrobat's reflexes, reports that he has personally smashed twenty-one tsetses. "Plus two assists," he adds. His feat earns him the nickname "Killer" for the rest of the trip.

But if the bites of the tsetse flies are the price of admission to the animals' world, we gratefully, eagerly pay it.

———————

"Any time now, we are expecting to see hundreds of thousands of wildebeests," says Dick. It's two p.m., and we're straddling Serengeti National Park and the edge of the Grumeti Reserves, one of the richest areas of the entire Serengeti ecosystem. My heart starts to pound. I'm longing to join the herd, perhaps the same

Blood on our vehicle's window (and Logan's iPad) testifies to Logan's prowess as Chief Tsetse Killer.

way the wildebeests long for the scent of rain and the first flush of green grass. We all feel the same.

"We'll go up on this rise and look for them," says Joshua.

We mount the hill and pop our heads through the roof. "Look around and see if you can spot the wildebeest migration," says Dick. We swing our field glasses—Joshua and Anna call them "the bins"—to our eyes and scan.

"No, those are bushes," says Joshua.

"Are those . . . ?" asks Liz.

"Nope," says Dick.

"What about . . . ?" I offer. But it's just more bushes.

There are no wildebeests in sight.

"They've flown the coop," announces Dick. "Oh dear."

"When they get moving, they can just disappear," agrees Joshua.

"But if it's anything like our last trip together," Roger reminds Dick, "we may still catch up with them up north." We are heading steadily northward until we reach the border with Kenya. But our trip is more than half over.

─────────────

After dinner, back at the lodge, tech wizard Roger succeeds in downloading Grant's tracking data from serengeti-tracker.org. It reveals that yesterday, one of his collared wildebeests was only a few miles east of us—we just missed him! But most of the other collared animals were at, past, or heading to Nyasarori, to our northeast.

"We're just a little bit behind them!" says Joshua. "So, do we have a target for tomorrow?"

Dick has gone to bed uncharacteristically early, beset with a cold he caught on the transatlantic flight. So in his absence, we pull out maps to try to plot our route. We discover there's just one problem: there are no roads between Nyasarori and our next camp, at Ikoma. "Where they seem to have gone is not accessible," notes Roger.

Joshua, Roger, and Logan pore over the map. Where are the wildebeests?

"Very uncooperative beasts," says Anna. What to do?

Joshua and Anna consult. Since there's no way to pry the wildebeests out of an inaccessible area, perhaps, in the morning, we will visit an area called Kirawira, a place where Dick often camped, famous for particularly huge crocodiles. "And if we leave early, we might see all the wildebeests who are the dregs of the migration," says Joshua.

"That could be pretty informative," says Anna. By the dregs, Joshua means the still-living casualties of the trek: animals who were left behind. Wounded, starving stragglers.

The thought is depressing. But Anna's right: it's an important part of the story of the migration. We need to understand the cost of the migration as well as its majesty.

Come evening, taunted by the trail of fresh hoof prints, exhausted from slapping flies, I try to steel myself for the lessons of the migration—even the sad ones.

Tsetse Flies

EVEN AS THEY BIT US, WE HAD TO ADMIRE THEM. TSETSE FLIES—SO NAMED for the word for "fly" in the Tswana language of South Arica—are tough and strong. They've been on earth for at least thirty-four million years (which scientists know from fossilized tsetse flies unearthed in Colorado!). And at one point in human history, conservationists called these bloodsucking insects "the best game wardens in Africa."

How can a bloodsucking fly be a friend to wild animals? The answer involves human mistakes, two deadly diseases, and how the African landscape was affected by both.

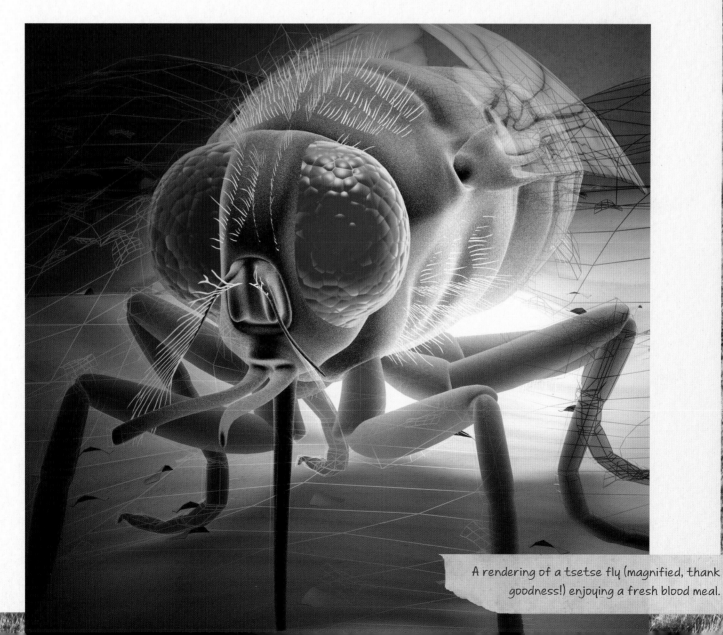

A rendering of a tsetse fly (magnified, thank goodness!) enjoying a fresh blood meal.

Tsetses have lived in Africa for a very long time, where they are hated not only for their painful bite but also for their ability to spread a parasite that causes the deadly human disease known as sleeping sickness. The parasite finds its way to the brain. Victims suffer fever, mood swings, and confusion. They can't sleep at night and can't stay awake by day. Without treatment, sleeping sickness is almost always fatal. (It can kill animals, too, but infected animals are more likely to survive.)

So where lots of tsetse flies lived, people did not. Most African people sensibly avoided living in or visiting tsetse-infested areas—especially woodlands and thorny scrub near waterways.

Tsetses were once scarce in East Africa. But everything changed when European colonists began to seize control of much of the African continent. In some cases, the invaders were deliberately cruel and selfish. But one far-reaching effect of colonization was completely unintentional. In the late 1880s, Italians imported Indian cattle to Somalia—not realizing the cows had a horrible disease.

This disease was a very different illness from sleeping sickness. The imported animals, who had seemed healthy at first, turned out to be infected with rinderpest—a German word that means "cattle plague." Known until then only in Europe and Asia, rinderpest is a contagious virus, related to measles. Rinderpest is not transmitted by insect bites, and doesn't afflict people. But it spreads among animals through direct contact—which in a herd happens all the time.

Rinderpest spread faster than wildfire across the African continent. The disease killed 95 percent of the cattle in East Africa in two years—along with countless other hoofed animals, including wildebeests. Without their cattle, pastoralists and farmers starved. Deprived of wild game, some lions turned to man-eating. Without grazers to keep the savanna open, many former grasslands grew up into woodland and thorny brush.

The absence of grazers created the perfect habitat for tsetse flies. Even though only one in one thousand flies carries sleeping sickness, so many flies thrived in this altered habitat that the disease became common. And the flies spread into new areas. People soon found many areas uninhabitable.

Therein lay the salvation of East Africa's wildlife—at least for a time.

Because if there's one thing worse for wildlife than biting flies, it's people—people who kill wild herbivores to eat them, people who kill predators because they compete with them, people who kill animals just to mount their heads on the wall. And the noxious humans wisely moved away from the disease-causing tsetses.

Once the wild animal population recovered from the rinderpest epidemic, elephants cleared much of the thorny brush away. Wildebeests and their entourage mowed and maintained the path to their migration. By the end of the nineteenth century and well into the twentieth, the Serengeti was once again a savanna paradise for animals. We have tsetse flies to thank for that!

Today, sleeping sickness is no longer a death sentence. The disease can be cured with drugs if detected early. And tsetse flies may be on the wane. They still frequent scrub and woodlands, especially near rivers. But scientists have now devised a way to reduce their numbers. University of Liverpool scientists figured out an ingenious way to trap the flies. We saw these traps often. They looked like bright-blue-and-black fabric boxes.

Turns out tsetse flies love bright blue—and when they circle the blue cloth, they hit poisoned netting inside and die within three minutes. And because most tsetse flies don't carry sleeping sickness, not every fly needs die to nearly eradicate the illness.

Cases of sleeping sickness are rapidly declining. During the most recent epidemic, in the late 1990s, an estimated three hundred thousand people were infected each year. In 2015 it caused around 3,500 deaths, down from 34,000 in 1990. Today, the human death toll is fewer than ten thousand each year.

Tsetse flies once saved the Serengeti. Now, it will be up to us.

Other Magnificent Migrants: Monarch Butterflies

IN THE MIDDLE OF MARCH, IN THE FOG-SHROUDED MOUNTAINS OF MEXICO'S Michoacán, the branches of fir trees seem swollen, as if wrapped in woolen sweaters. Sunrise reveals the truth: not wool, but wings, clothe these trees. A rustle sweeps through the forest, as wave after wave of flame-orange wings spread open—the wings of three hundred million monarch butterflies. The monarch's is the largest, longest, most spectacular, most highly evolved migration of any insect on earth.

Researchers consider these creatures the world's most astounding navigators—because none of the migrants have ever completed the round-trip journey before. It takes them four generations to do so.

Consider the transformations these animals undergo before they even begin the arduous migration. A monarch caterpillar grows to two thousand times its size at birth

in August. And then when it forms a chrysalis, in two weeks it dissolves into a bag of fluid—which reassembles itself into a completely new life form: a butterfly.

In September, over a billion monarchs take off from their northerly birth sites in the United States and Canada to head south toward Mexico. After nine hundred hours of flying, in late October, they arrive in Mexico and Southern California—to the same grove, and in some cases on the same tree, that their forefathers clung to the year before. For five months they cluster together in a sort of trance, until the lengthening daylight awakens them and inspires them to mate. This leading generation flies five hundred miles in three weeks, to the American South, where they lay eggs on milkweed plants and die.

Their children—and their children's children—grow from caterpillars, pupate, emerge, and fly north. They fan out across North America. By August, the fourth generation—sometimes known as the super generation—will be born. These monarchs will live ten times longer than their parents, and these are the insects who fly back to overwinter in Mexico.

How do they do it? They certainly don't learn from their parents. Researchers are studying how these insects might use the angle of the sun along the horizon in combination with an internal body clock to maintain a steady flight path. But most believe this would have to be combined with some other kind of clue. Like loggerhead sea turtles, they may also use a magnetic compass, registering the angle made by the earth's magnetic field and the ground.

Some fear the migration might end even before it can be understood. Illegal logging in Mexico and erratic weather patterns caused by global climate disruption threaten the butterflies' survival.

But most serious is the threat to the monarchs' food. Monarch caterpillars feed on a single plant—milkweed—which renders them unpalatable to predators. Once, milkweed was so abundant in farmers' fields along monarchs' migration routes that every kid used to catch the floating downy seeds and wish on them before releasing them back into the air. Today, crops genetically engineered to withstand applications of an herbicide, Roundup, allow farmers to wipe out virtually every single milkweed plant on their land.

Chapter Seven

Liz couldn't sleep. Even though our quarters at Mbalageti were the most luxurious we'd experienced yet—no tents this time, but individual chalets with bathtubs and hot running water—she was up, tossing and turning, scratching the many tsetse bites on her legs.

So she was the first to hear it: soft and distant at first, then closer and more resonant. She stayed up all night listening. "Neeh! Noo! Neeh! NOO! NEEH! NOO!"

By five a.m., the voices are so loud they wake all of us. They sound like a cross between a herd of mooing cows and a chorus of giant bullfrogs. The calls surround us like waves in the ocean. We look out over the plains from our individual balconies and see them in the distance, streaming like lines of ants.

"*That's* where they all are!" says Anna.

We gulp down breakfast and hurry to the Land Cruiser. "There's a steady stream of them coming out of the bush," says Dick, "and they keep coming. There's a good chance they're trekking to water." He's observed that wildebeests tend to go to water after the early-morning feeding peak, and in the middle of the day.

So we head to the Grumeti River. Our ob-jective is simple, says Dick. "Find wildebeests. Watch the migration. Observe the rut."

In the distance, we see big lines of gnus heading in both directions: northeast, toward the Mara River, and southwest. "It's not uncommon for the migration to reverse direction," Dick reminds us.

"Look! There's heaps more filing in," says Anna.

The calls throb and swell all around us. But Dick says the surround sound can get even louder and more immersive. "There were times," he remembers, "when, sitting in my Land Rover surrounded by wildebeests, I sometimes felt I was drowning in sound."

"At peak calling times," he wrote in *The Gnu's World,* "with thousands of bulls producing their basso grunts and honks, the air reverberated and pulsated, against a background roar that reminded me of heavy surf breaking against a rocky headland." No wonder he named it the Big Hum. What's perhaps most amazing about the Big Hum is that these are not the voices of all the wildebeests combined. It's the voices of the adult males alone. Though all wildebeests, even the calves, can vocalize loudly, Dick noticed early in his studies that only the males produced this deep, resonant chorus, and only during the rut.

The sound reminded him of thousands of croaking male frogs he'd hear back home in New Hampshire each spring. That gave him an idea. Other scientists had already established that the frog chorus stimulated females to produce eggs and mate. Dick wondered: Could this be the case with wildebeests, too?

In 2003, he was able to test his theory. With two other scientists and their staff, Dick supervised the darting and capture of eighteen female wildebeests. They were detained in a large pasture so that the scientists could collect their dung and analyze their sex hormones. Then the cows were divided into three groups. The first group was introduced to a handsome bull wildebeest. A second group got to hear Dick's recordings of the Big Hum. A control group was isolated from both the actual male wildebeest and the sounds. Measurements of the females' hormones showed that the Big Hum caused almost as big a spike in reproductive hormones as the presence of the Real Thing! And because the researchers purposely conducted the experiment three weeks earlier than the migratory population experienced the actual rutting season, the study showed that more than just the calendar was at work.

Dick and his colleagues proved that the Big Hum is the "mood music" that helps synchronize the rut. These thousands upon thousands of male voices ensure that 90 percent of the adult females—some 750,000 cows—conceive their babies during this brief, roughly three-week period. The Big Hum guarantees that most wildebeest calves will be born at about the same time, eight and a half months later—so many that even the hundreds of predators that trail the babies migrating with their mothers couldn't possibly eat them all. The Big Hum is a survival mechanism that protects the wildebeests' future. It's the soundtrack to the biggest party on earth.

And we're about to crash the party.

A strong, young bull stands triumphantly on a little mound, head held high. He's surrounded by ten cows who are enjoying the welcome cool beneath the canopy of a spreading acacia. "This chap has it made in the shade," Dick jokes approvingly. Not only does the site offer respite from the sun's harsh rays; this smart male has staked out this territory only a few hundred yards from the cool drinking water of the river. Convenience plus comfort: location, location, location.

Not every bull enjoys such success. During the 1980 rut, of 513 territorial males Dick surveyed, only 116 of them actually had any females on the territory they were so zealously promoting and guarding at the moment Dick spotted them. That's just one out of five. That shows how difficult it is to both attract and—importantly—hold a herd on your territory. For

Having wisely chosen a territory beneath a shady tree, a wildebeest bull (head and shoulders above the rest) gets lucky with one of the ladies.

to do the male any good, the females need to stay long enough to become receptive to mating and ready to conceive a calf.

Why does a bull need a whole herd of ladies, and not just one female at a time? As with people, a crowd attracts an even bigger crowd. "You could almost liken the successful bull to a duck hunter deploying a spread of decoys to lure the desired quarry—a female in heat—to land in his spread," Dick wrote in *The Gnu's World*. But like migrating ducks on a pond, a bull's herd won't stay on even the most enticing patch of ground for very long—and neither will he. Soon, the migratory urge overcomes them, and everyone moves on.

We're quite near the river now, and can see

where hundreds of thousands of hooves have recently churned the soil. We see wildebeests to the left of us, wildebeests ahead, wildebeests behind. But those behind us are still. They seem to be waiting. "We should move," says Joshua. "We may be stopping them."

We cross a bridge to a spot where we can watch the animals without disturbing them. The wildebeests behind us move forward now, entering the river's brown water, some up to their sloping shoulders. Some pause to drink. But suddenly, the water ripples. Instantly everyone rushes to turn back. They run out of the water panicked, the whites of their eyes showing their terror.

Their fear could be well-founded. The

brown water could easily conceal a crocodile. The Nile croc is Africa's largest reptile, with one of the world's strongest bites, a force calculated at five thousand pounds per square inch.

We hold our breath, expecting to see a huge head emerge from the water. But Roger, who'd been looking up to watch three black-and-white colobus monkeys in a tree, realizes the source of the ripples: it's only the splash of a stream of pee let loose by nervous monkeys overhead.

"Better safe than sorry" would be a good motto for the wildebeests crossing water. "Give a wildebeest a choice between drinking from a clear, flowing stream in the forest, and a nasty, alkaline pool in the open, they'll choose the alkaline pool—even if it's so alkaline the animals will be poisoned from drinking it," Dick tells us. "They'll *always* choose the open. Avoiding predators is that important."

Avoiding individual predators—including poachers with guns and snares—is a major reason that the various armies of wildebeests

Black-and-white colobus monkeys make their home high in the trees, eating leaves, fruit, flowers, and bark.

choose different routes on their migration each year. Grant's collared zebras and wildebeests both behave the same way when they encounter areas of high poaching: "Both species attempt to exit the area as soon as possible," Dick found, "by moving a long way and in straight lines, regardless of food. It appears these animals can detect risky areas and respond accordingly."

Water crossings are particularly dangerous. But sometimes the risk simply cannot be avoided. The Mara River flows along at the border between Tanzania and Kenya. Despite their good instincts, more than sixty thousand wildebeests are killed each year crossing this single waterway. As the wildebeests arrive, the predators move toward the river's bank and wait for them.

It's tragic for the individual wildebeests who are killed. But the migrating wildebeests sustain the Serengeti ecosystem by both their lives and their deaths. Migrations—of all species—create superabundance. Because the migrants' travels allow them to take advantage of fresh, high-quality food, animals who migrate often enjoy a richer and more varied diet than members of the same species who stay behind. That's why migratory animals can become ten times more numerous than members of the same species who do not migrate.

In such extreme numbers, migrants like wildebeests powerfully affect the landscape, and the other creatures who depend on it. And the migration is not just felt by the animals and plants on the land. It importantly nourishes waterways too: a study published in 2017 on the Serengeti's ecosystem showed that the thousands of migrating wildebeests who die during water crossings feed everyone from crocs to hippos (yes, hippos will occasionally eat meat!), affecting species from fish to water plants to aquatic microorganisms.

Yale researcher Amanda Subalusky found that the wildebeests who fall victim to crocs, hippos, or drowning profoundly enrich the entire watershed. "Hundreds of birds and crocodiles and fish and hyenas and mongoose are benefitting," she discovered. Beneath the water's surface, bones from the thousands of bodies act like slow-release fertilizer capsules that feed plants, which in turn feed and shelter fish, snails, and microorganisms, for *seven years* as they dissolve. Her study, published in the journal *Proceedings of the National Academy of Sciences,* showed that a wildebeest herd can influence even a watery ecosystem dramatically, and in a way that few people realized before.

Here, by this small crossing, two marabou storks sail over us, close enough that we can see their pink pouches, like giant double chins, wobbling to and fro in the air. Looking like lugubrious, balding undertakers, these storks are scavengers, and they soon are lunging at some fat, ropy-looking material on the ground. We realize these are intestines. And we know whose they are. Yesterday morning, when we passed by this same spot, we heard from other travelers

Vultures gather to feast upon the fallen. In the background, a lone marabou stork, also a scavenger, hopes for scraps.

that we'd just missed glimpsing a leopard. Later that afternoon, we'd spotted a lost calf, starving, calling for his mother.

The leopard must have heard the baby's desperate calls. Maybe the leopard was a female with young of her own. In ending the calf's suffering, she fed herself, perhaps her cubs, as well as these storks. The calf may have nourished many other lives as well.

⸻

Driving slowly, Joshua takes us along the river's edge. Wildebeests thunder by with zebras. Wildebeests rest beneath acacias. Wildebeests

trot alongside warthogs. One bull canters in circles, keeping his cows and calves from leaving his territory. Another rushes out from his territory toward a file of new females, trying to draw their attention to his tree. He chases off a neighboring male. But meanwhile his own females start wandering off, and he has to round them up.

This time of year, notes Dick, the males' stripes are particularly bold, their posture especially proud. "You can tell from five kilometers away that's a territorial male. Look at him!" says Dick admiringly, pointing straight ahead of us. "Very statuesque. He's a prime bull, all right." The handsome fellow drives his cows and calves back to the shade of a tree and stamps emphatically, as if to say "Look! Stay *here!* You're not going to find a better spot than this!"

The action is fast all around us. Yet another male takes a step forward and stamps. One to our left is still on his knees from a fight with a neighbor. His rival has just run off to herd his wandering females back to his territory—but on his way he encounters a third male, who horns the ground menacingly.

Dick, despite his miserable airplane cold, is elated. He breaks into song. To the tune of "Joshua Fit the Battle of Jericho," he sings "Joshua Finds the Giant Herds of Wildebeest." A single bull stands in a little grove of trees, offering luxuriant shade. "He should get a nice herd here," says Dick. He's happy for him.

Straight ahead, two males converge in the road, right in front of our Land Cruiser. The bull on our left touches his head to his neighbor's rump. The other urinates; his neighbor grimaces, accessing his vomeronasal organ to sample his rival's hormones. Suddenly, both drop to their knees and smash horns!

Then, as if on cue, having discharged their duty at the appointed time and place, they each rise and trot back to their designated territories, about a thousand yards apart. They resume advertising their property.

Our track departs from the river, and we find ourselves back on the plains. One male wildebeest has attracted a useless harem beneath his tree. They're all zebras! "What is he going to do with *those?*" asks Logan. Another bull has amassed a little crowd of seven comely wildebeest cows. But mostly, as the males stand stalwart, the females file past with their young. From horizon to horizon we see wildebeests. "Even a panorama doesn't do it justice," says Roger, taking photos. "And yesterday it was so empty!"

Much of the grass has been eaten down. The few, little trees have been whiplashed by horns. Yet, still, they are coming, coming from all directions, the females seeking food, water, and shade, the males seeking sex. Different goals, but united in their longing: another day of life, and another and another, with its juicy savors, its comforting company, its transforming journeys.

One male stands near the road, shaking his head. His right horn hangs by a shred of flesh, broken nearly off. "Imagine the impact it would take to do that!" says Dick. Quietly we all imagine the passion, the force, the pain. "One of the incredible things I noticed in Grumeti," Dick continues, "was a broken horn that broke the wildebeest's skull, exposing the brain." And yet that animal, like this one, still stood on his mound, brave, patient, and hopeful.

⸻

"We're in the midst of a major migration through here, no question," says Dick. The grass is grazed to nubs, the bushes bashed to oblivion, the ground littered with manure from the wil-

Nearly broken off in combat, this bull's dangling horn must have been agonizing. He bends his neck toward his flank, trying to dislodge it.

debeests and dozens of species of camp followers. And there are signs of the casualties, too: we spot about fifty vultures on the ground, with more and more, their legs extended like landing gear, tumbling out of the sky. Dick identifies the three species we see here: The Rüppell's griffon is the largest. One researcher calculated that this species alone cleans up more than thirteen thousand pounds of decaying remains from the Serengeti each year. The white-backed vultures are even more common, with their black faces, brown plumage, and distinctive white feathers on the wings and back. The smallest vulture is the scruffy-looking hooded vulture. But all of them are sizeable and imposing, standing over two feet tall with wingspans spanning more than five feet. These big birds march in on strong legs, hissing and swaggering. Many guides believe these vultures, with their heavy beaks, rip through the animal's hide so other animals could feed from the carcass. But Dick knows this isn't true. "Actually they don't get involved until most of the flesh is already exposed," he says. "Two years ago in Etosha, we passed a zebra

carcass that had not been opened. Three hours later we drove by to see it had attracted hundreds of vultures. But all of them were waiting. None were eating. They were all waiting for a mammal to come and open it for them."

Someone must have done this for these vultures, because those closest to the carcass are lunging and grabbing, their naked heads and necks striking at the opened flesh. This is why vultures (and marabou storks, who are also scavengers) are bald: Who wants to sully head feathers with rotting meat? With all the grabbing and tugging, the corpse jiggles back and forth spasmodically. "It's moving almost as if it's alive," Gary remarks. Meanwhile, more vultures fall

from the sky. The scene inspires Roger to add a new line to Dick's "Joshua Fit the Battle" parody: "And the vultures come tumbling down!" We all break into song afresh as we turn off the road to join up with the river again.

We drive on, happy, singing—until we hear a loud *clunk*. Joshua notices the car won't go into gear. We all get out. The guys inspect the front.

But Liz, who has hopped out of the car to stretch, wanders to the back of the vehicle. She notices fluid has spilled all over the left rear wheel, and that the bolts on the hubcap have sheared off.

It looks like car blood. The diagnosis: the left

half axle from the wheel differential—which turns the wheel—is no longer attached to the wheel. The fluid, the differential oil, is draining out. If this continues the entire differential will seize and the car will no longer be able to move.

This is disturbing news. It's two forty-five, the hottest part of the day, and we happen to be marooned in a pocket of particularly busy tsetse flies. It could be hours before a ranger, or another safari vehicle, stops to retrieve our party and return us to the Mbalageti Lodge—then more time till the car can be towed, and then fixed. All the while, we risk falling farther behind the wildebeests . . .

But Joshua, Anna, Roger, and Logan know just what to do. "We need something to keep the oil from draining out," says Anna. Roger and Logan select a yellow-and-blue SEE BUY FLY bag from our layover at the Amsterdam airport. They attach it to the wheel with a rubber hair band fished from my backpack and a spare inner tube from the back of the car. With the touch of a button, Joshua locks the wounded differential drive to the still-working one. "We'll game-drive back to camp," Joshua announces cheerfully.

Along the way, we spot two territorial male gnus, each having attracted his own herd of la-

In the absence of spare parts, the team used a plastic bag and a rubber band.

dies. One bull stands beneath a large, lovely sausage tree—so named for its long, sausage-like fruit—offering ample shade to about forty females.

But the other bull's success is even more impressive. He's standing beneath the most pathetic acacia imaginable: only four feet tall, its three branches offering no visible shade, it reminds us of the Charlie Brown Christmas tree. Yet beneath its scraggly limbs, he has managed to amass at least twenty females.

With such a little tree, how did he attract anyone?

"It's not about size," says Roger. "It's how you use it!"

"He must have a great personality," says Anna.

We laugh, but soon are sobered. As the sun begins to drop, we pass the broken-horned male again. His horn still hangs by one agonizing thread. Flies swarm the bloody wound. It's at least ninety-five degrees in the blazing sun. Yet despite the heat, despite the flies, despite the pain, here he remains, with the unwavering dedication of a soldier, standing on his hot, treeless territory.

How long will he stay? Dick's studies have found that a bull might hold on to his plot of land from as short as fifteen minutes to as long as several weeks. "There are bulls who stay

Size matters: A big tree attracts the ladies.

put even after all the wildebeest armies have passed!" Dick says. Even when the herds have mown the pasture to nubs, some bulls remain behind. Why don't these diehards move on? Come evening, if the group has been feeding in taller grass, females in search of a safer place to spend the night might come back. After all, bare ground can't conceal predators. "So even this tactic might well pay off," says Dick. Even our broken-horned friend may still have reason for hope.

As the sky streaks with red, a long wildebeest file continues to our right, and ahead of them in the distance we see thousands more. Bulls under their trees watch them go by, and call: "Neh! Noo! Come back! Come back!" And perhaps they will, tonight or tomorrow.

Just before we reach the lodge, Dick just can't help but pull a prank. Passing a territorial male, he calls out the window to him: "Neh!! Noo!" The male stares at Dick at what appears to us to be stricken disbelief. *Don't tell me I have to compete with you, too?*

Snares: The Cruelest Death

"OH NO. WHAT'S WRONG WITH THAT GUY? LOOK AT HIS LEG . . ."

Anna knew immediately what was wrong. Behind his left rear leg, the limping young male wildebeest trailed nine yards of wire, attached to a broken branch. The illegally set snare sliced ever deeper into his flesh.

He'd fallen victim to one of the cruelest, and most widespread, of poachers' weapons. Cheap, lightweight, easy to make, the typical snare is nothing more than a length of wire, often harvested from old tires, attached to a heavy rock or tree, and ending in a loop formed by a slip knot. It's set where an animal might walk. It's ruthlessly effective: if an animal steps in it, or sniffs it, and tries to move away, tension within the loop slides the knot along the wire and pulls it tight. Sometimes the animal breaks free. But the knot continues to tighten. Without help, the animal almost always dies.

Anna and I witnessed the tragedy one afternoon when we took a research vehicle to look for herds, while the rest of the group took a different route.

Narrowing and swelling on this zebra's neck bear witness to the ravages of a snare.

Anna immediately grabbed her cell. "When we see a snared animal, we call the warden and whatever vet we can get a hold of, and stay with the animal till the vet arrives," she explained as she dialed.

"Dammit! No network!"

Now, what?

Anna and two veterinarians from the Tanzania Wildlife Research Institute attempt to remove a snare from the leg of a baby elephant. The mother has also been sedated for the safety of the capture team.

Sadly, there was nothing we could do. Though the snare was a death sentence, for the moment, the wildebeest was still too fast for us to catch, and too strong for us to help, without a dart gun.

"Poor guy! Oh, buddy," she said to the young male . . . *"Pole,"* she whispered to him in Swahili, the word for "sorry." She turned to me. "I only hope he goes quickly . . ."

We clenched our teeth in anger as we turned our eyes away.

A recent study by the World Conservation Monitoring Centre and the United Nations' conservation program estimates that, just in the western Serengeti alone, snares like this doom an estimated two hundred thousand animals of dozens of species to agonizing, prolonged deaths.

Anna has seen it too many times before. These snares are set for bushmeat, but also catch species people won't even eat. So many elephants have had trunks severed by snares, she said, that "some people think it's a new disease that makes elephants' trunks fall off. I assure them, no—it's snares."

Anna will never forget the two-and-a-half-year-old elephant who had a snare caught on his foot for months. He'd been hanging around by one of the entrance gates to Serengeti National Park. She and others had tried many times to help the youngster, but it's a difficult and dangerous operation—not least because rescuers need to drive his entire herd away in order to dart and treat the baby.

But finally, Anna and a team of vets were able to step in and help. By then the snare had worked itself deep into the little elephant's flesh. "When the snare came off, there was a geyser of blood," she remembers—blood that she knew would draw predators. Even though Anna was running out of water, she stayed with him all night. She shooed off hungry hyenas. And her young companion seemed to understand she was there to protect him. "I'd doze off and he'd trumpet, and come toward my car," she remembers.

In the morning, she found his group. With the help of a ranger, the family was reunited. "He was such a little trooper!" she said of the baby.

But the story did not end well. Anna was called away for some work in Botswana. When she came back, she learned he had died. Because of his wounds, he couldn't keep up with his family. He was eaten by a lion.

These young ostriches have probably known each other since they were in their eggs. They hatched from a communal nest, with a number of different parents.

Chapter Eight

After spending a second, blissful day among the herds at Mbalageti, today we head for one of the highlights of the trip: the Grumeti and Ikorongo Reserves, where both Dick and Anna have worked for years.

"It's the very essence of the Serengeti ecosystem," says Dick, "and it should be covered in wildebeests, zebras, gazelles." This may be the best-protected area that the wildebeests visit on their migration.

Though technically game reserves (where controlled hunting is allowed) ever since 2002, these blocks of hunting concessions have been leased from the Tanzanian government by billionaire philanthropist Paul Tudor-Jones II. The former futures trader is using his money to restore degraded land and protect and restore its

animals. The reserves' 540 square miles—bigger than Grand Teton National Park, and about a tenth the size of the entire Serengeti—are extensively patrolled by well-trained, well-equipped, dedicated rangers. And because Dick and Anna know the owner personally, as their guests, we will not be confined to the tracks. We can go off-road. Here we can get closer to the animals than anywhere else we'll go.

The trip there will be a splendid game drive, Joshua promises. The morning air reverberates with the Big Hum, mixed with the braying of migrating zebras. As we drive east toward the river crossing, it seems every space is packed with journeying animals, strong, graceful, and determined. Some head northeast, the same direction they traveled yesterday morning. Other groups are moving west, pacing briskly and swishing their long tails. Dick tells us they are coming from the open areas to converge at the river for their morning drink.

We drive on, and at nine, before the sun has even risen very high, it's already hot enough that the wildebeests seek the shade of trees. We stop to watch about eighty vultures on a carcass. Gary says they sound like a gaggle of cackling witches. The big Rüppell's griffon has the heaviest bill, but the white-backed vultures seem in charge of the prize, which is little more than ribs and skin. Lappet-faced vultures, with their fluffy wings on the ground, look like old men sitting in overstuffed armchairs. White-backed vultures are squabbling among themselves, pull-ing and picking at bits of flesh, hissing, cackling, their long naked necks craning like snakes rising out of an empty robe.

Nearby, two other lappet-faced vultures, having feasted on the carcass, are in the mood for love. "He took her to a fancy restaurant," says Gary, "and now he deserves a kiss." They groom each other delicately. One gently nibbles the other's breast feathers, while the mate holds the wings slightly open, welcoming, trusting.

By nine thirty we are crossing an open plain. It's deserted. The wildebeests are gone. Soon we'll exit Serengeti National Park, and take a road whose western extension skirts Lake Victoria, the largest lake in Africa and the reservoir of the Nile.

We drive and drive. Ahead, lush trees mark the course of the Grumeti River. Here long lines of trekking wildebeests cross the road, stretching farther than we can see. We wait ten minutes while they pass. An hour's drive later, we can see they've been through—cropped grass, trampled earth, pebbles of dung—but again, the wildebeests are gone. I get out to smell the earth where they passed. I kneel like a pilgrim facing a holy site and inhale. The smell is pungent but not unpleasant: warm and vaguely oily.

Pursued by tsetse flies, we continue on. There's much to see: a trio of male giraffes. Eleven young ostriches. They're all who remain from a crèche of hatchlings sired by different parents that once numbered perhaps thirty or forty, Dick tells us. Almost nothing can take

If we can't see the wildebeests, at least I can smell them!

Looking into trees . . .

down a grown ostrich, whose kick can kill a cheetah. But baby ostriches provide food for many predators. Vultures circle above us. Warthogs trot by, their slender, tuft-tipped tails held jauntily high.

When we stop for a picnic lunch, Logan stands on our Land Cruiser to examine the inside of a hanging weaver bird's nest—and spots a striped pattern, then a swiveling eye. A chameleon, horrified to see such a monster peering at him, drops to the ground—where Joshua grabs him so we can examine him more closely. With eyes atop cone-shaped turrets that can move independently, the chameleon can look in two different directions at once. He makes his living hunting insects that he captures on his extendable, sticky tongue—a tongue twice the length of his body. Chameleon and humans examine each other carefully for a few minutes before

Joshua gently releases the lizard back up in the tree.

Finally we pass through the gates of the ranger post to the Grumeti Reserves. Ranger Kokan Adiel, uniformed in khaki, greets Dick and Anna warmly.

"How was your safari?" Kokan asks me politely. I tell him of the river of wildebeests we saw at Mbalageti. "But we're so excited, because we know even *more* animals will be *here!*" I answer enthusiastically.

"Yes, there are so many they are uncountable!" he says. My heart races.

"But," Kokan continues, "there are remarkably few wildebeests here at the moment. Three weeks ago, there were a lot of them," he tells us. "But now, they have all gone north."

The wildebeests have vanished. Again.

. . . yields a new friend. This chameleon's eyes can move independently, and he can grasp with hands, feet, and tail.

De-Snaring the Serengeti

BY THE TIME THEY FOUND HER, THE ZEBRA HAD NEARLY SUFFOCATED. **P**AN-icked by the wire closing around her neck, the animal had run around and around the tree to which the snare was tethered, until she was smack up against the trunk, choking and terrified.

"We had to cut the tree down in order to get the wires loose," Abraham Saidea told me. The desperate animal tried to bite and kick him and the others on his team. "But we were able to save the zebra alive and release it. We cut it loose. It was a special occasion to see it run and join its herd."

Abraham, sixty-three, is the leader of a special team of eight men recruited from local villages in the Serengeti to staff a new program, founded in 2017, that is de-snaring the Serengeti.

Team leader Abraham Saidea and his men collected 1,600 illegal snares in their first month of patrols.

Working in concert with Tanzania National Parks, the Serengeti De-Snaring Programme is organized by the Frankfurt Zoological Society and financed with money from hotel owners and tour operators. Many of the men on the de-snaring team are former poachers themselves; the program uses their knowledge and experience to find the snares and remove them. The men, in turn, receive good pay and no longer face the threat of being arrested, fined, or jailed.

Abraham, a former park ranger, was enticed out of retirement to lead the team. During his forty years as a ranger, he came to know the ravages of these snares all too well. But he had other duties as a ranger; he couldn't devote all his time to ridding the park of the scourge. Now he can—and the results are jaw-dropping.

The day Abraham and I spoke, I was back in the States, and he had just completed a ten-day patrol with his men. During that short time, they collected six hundred illegal snares. "That's six hundred animals you may have saved in ten days!" I said in astonishment. "Yes," he said quietly. "It's important to me to save even one life."

The snare around this impala's neck will continue to tighten.

In the first month of the program alone, they recovered 1,600 snares, found 140 trapped animals, and released 21 animals alive—most of them wildebeests. During the first eight months of the program, between its start in mid-April and the day we spoke over the phone in November, the team had removed 8,503 snares.

Working alongside a current national park ranger, the team has discovered dozens of poachers' camps. Extensive surveys conducted recently by the Frankfurt Zoological Society found that most poachers' families raise chickens, goats, and sheep for protein. They don't depend on bushmeat to survive. They set their snares to sell that meat for quick profits. (Pound for pound, bushmeat at the market sells for more than chicken but less than beef.) Many locals, whose ancestors had been free for generations to hunt game without restriction, resented the laws passed to protect the animals. Before the de-snaring program, poaching animals for meat was easy, and there was relatively little chance of being caught.

But that's changing—at least in areas where the de-snaring program has begun. On their last patrol, Abraham told me, they took in six poachers. If convicted, the criminals can be sentenced to fines and jail time.

When the program first started, said Abraham, his team would find the snares, take them away—and discover that the poachers had simply put out new traps again the next day. But word is spreading. "We hope they eventually stop putting the traps out," says Abraham.

It's going to take a lot more work to get to that point, he realizes. Tanzanian park officials, the Frankfurt Zoological Society, and hotel and safari operators (who depend on wildlife for their income) know that too. That's why they're hoping to expand the de-snaring program to eight teams, in order to cover larger areas in the Serengeti.

The morning we talked, it was evening in the Serengeti, and Abraham was on his way home for a few days to see his wife, nine kids, and four grandchildren. He's grateful his new job earns good money for his family. But his work brings them more than just a paycheck.

"It's important we save the wildlife for future generations," he said, "so they will be able to see and be proud of what Tanzania has. Our wildlife is something we inherited, and we need to care for, for our children and grandchildren."

In dust kicked up by millions of hooves, as a herd of wildebeests passes, elands look at us curiously.

Chapter Nine

In the morning, at the gate, we transfer from our Land Cruiser to an open vehicle owned by the Grumeti Reserves. With no sides or top, it's ideal for viewing wildlife. And even if the wildebeests have moved on, there's much to see here, Dick promises.

As usual, he's right. A river of zebras appears in back of us, golden dust rising from their hooves. Ahead, large herds of hundreds of Cape buffaloes congregate. We can see thousands of Tommies and Grant's gazelles. And here, for the first time, we find large groups of one of Africa's most magnificent antelopes: elands.

These largest and most ox-like of Africa's antelopes are impressive and striking, with tawny coats punctuated with several white stripes, black garters on the upper forelegs, and spiral-

ing horns in both sexes that face backwards. The one-ton males sport massive necks and enlarged dewlaps, folds of loose skin hanging from the neck and chin. But despite their bulk, elands are nonetheless incredible high-jumpers. An adult can jump effortlessly over the six-foot shoulders of a neighbor; and a youngster, Dick wrote in his *Behavior Guide,* "can sail effortlessly over a three meter high fence [that's nearly 10 feet!] from a standing jump."

Liz is elated. When she lived with the San Bushmen of Namibia, she'd spot these magnificent antelopes from time to time, but only five or six at once, and only at a distance. "They knew how far an arrow could travel," she remembers—and they always stayed at that remove, because that's how the San hunted them.

Once a poisoned arrow hit an eland, the hunter could often outrun the animal until the poison did its work. Elands can't run fast for long; they're built for jumping, not racing. Elands were prized prey for the Bushmen. Unlike most antelopes, who are lean, elands store fat, making their meat sweet and juicy. And as Liz explains, because of its life-giving calories, to hunter-gatherers, "fat is life."

"These elands are in superb condition," Dick pronounces. There are more than a hundred of them, and the normally shy animals are calmly strolling less than seventy-five yards away from us. Here they know they are well protected from arrows, snares, and guns, thanks to conservationist Paul Tudor-Jones's sophisticated antipoaching patrols.

Normally wary, the elands we met at Grumeti and Ikorongo Reserves were extraordinarily calm.

Because of these dedicated, brave, and well-funded men, the Grumeti and Ikorongo Reserves host animals we haven't seen before. One focus of Tudor-Jones's conservation effort is to reintroduce animals who have gone locally extinct due to human interference—like the wild dogs who were wiped out from this corner of the Serengeti because of rabies and distemper spread by local people's domesticated dogs. We catch a glimpse of one of the two packs of these critically endangered canids who've been introduced here. A TV crew is filming them, so we watch at a distance. But we're thrilled to see six of these athletic creatures, with their distinctive, giant, rounded ears and boldly patterned coats of black, white, and tan, lying in the muddy shade beneath a thorn tree—until a hyena approaches, and they instantly disperse.

There are even rhinos here, though we don't get to see them. Due to poaching for their horns (in Asia, it's widely and incorrectly believed that powder ground from their horns provides an aphrodisiac), the black rhino is one of the most endangered animals in Africa. A big bull was transported from Ngorongoro in 2015, and was soon joined by females from South Africa. They're in a spacious and heavily guarded enclosure for captive breeding and later release.

As we drive on, the abundance of wildlife astounds us. A herd of about fifty impalas rushes by. We encounter a huge file of zebras, fat and healthy, trekking to water, the senior mare in the lead. Zebras keep flowing past us for eight minutes, until we finally spot the stallion bring-

Rhinos, too, have been reintroduced at Grumeti.

ing up the rear. Nearby is another herd of more than a hundred Cape buffaloes, the formidable males weighing in at 1,500 pounds. Plastered on their broad heads, both males and females boast horns curved like an oversize handlebar mustache, forming a massive shield across the forehead. Though the tendency to gore people gives them a nasty reputation, this mixed herd—males, females, and offspring together—seems as calm as cattle.

Both of these species enjoy the company of wildebeests. We may find large groups of gnus yet, our driver, Baraka, tells us.

"This game drive is already more fruitful than we expected," says Dick. "Who knows? We may see wildebeests rutting!"

A minute later, it seems our hopes may be fulfilled. "Territorial bull on the left!" Dick calls. "Wildebeests may be crossing at the Grumeti River." We can see its shores looming ahead, thick with shady trees, shrubs, and vines.

Sure enough, there are wildebeests here—though not great herds. As we approach, we can feel their tension. "Because predators wait near water," Dick reminds us, "everyone's on maximum alert."

But it's more than that. Something else is wrong.

We get closer, and now we see why the wildebeests are worried. That male has a swollen knee. This calf is limping. A female, her udder swollen with milk, calls for her missing calf. A mother wildebeest will continue to call for her baby even if she saw it being killed by a predator, Dick tells us. "They can't help it," he says, "it's hardwired." It sounds crazy, but we humans do this too. I've done it myself: for months after her death, I'd speak aloud the name of my dead dog in private moments of grief—even though I knew she couldn't hear.

A few dozen yards later, a calf lies dead. A bull has a broken horn. Yet another has a broken leg. Why are there so many dead and injured?

"These," Dick realizes, "are the stragglers." Anna calls them "the walking wounded."

The grass in many areas is shaved to the nubs. Bare earth, hoof prints, trails. "There's been one heck of a lot of animals through here," says Dick. "This was one major migration. We are just seeing the end."

These are the lost, the broken, the doomed: A bull hops on three legs. Two crippled calves limp behind a female, who is probably neither one's mother. They are hoping she might adopt them, but this seldom happens, Dick tells us. Their fate is probably that of the next calf we see: vultures are feeding on its carcass. "Sometimes vultures take the eyeballs out while the calf is still alive," Anna tells us.

The migration leaves in its wake the heartbreaking carnage we associate with war zones: wounds, starvation, orphans, broken bones. Another territorial bull stands under his tree holding up his right rear leg. The tube-shaped bone in the lower leg, between the fetlock and the knee, is broken. "Oh my God," says Dick,

Lionesses sack out under a shady tree.

stricken. "That's broken terribly. That one won't recover."

Just imagining his pain is excruciating. How can he even think about advertising and defending his territory? How can he even go on? And yet he does—as do the injured females and the orphaned calves.

Dick once saw a hartebeest being eaten alive by wild dogs. "He was just kind of calmly looking around" during the ordeal. "Prey species seem to go into a shock reaction," Dick observes. "That sort of wound may actually produce a natural anesthetic."

Liz shares the story of a San girl she knew when her family lived in the Namibian desert. The girl was far from their encampment. Her leg was caught in a leghold trap someone had

set for a hyena. Many hours later, an uncle saw her. He didn't know how to open the trap. He couldn't get the trap off—but he gave her a spear to help her balance as she stood on her one good leg. Only the person who set the trap knew how to release her. So the uncle went to find him.

"The girl had been in this leghold trap for hours and hours," Liz tells us. "She had a bad wound. But when we saw her, and came to treat her, she wasn't even gritting her teeth. She was just calmly chatting with us, as if there were nothing wrong."

Another man Liz knew when her family lived in the Namibian desert was bitten by a puff adder—one of the most toxic vipers on earth. "The man eventually lost the leg," Liz remembers. "But after the bite, he was perfectly calm."

To most of us today, pain and panic twine tight. And fear does have its place, biologically speaking. It spurs the release of brain chemicals that constitute our natural alarm system. Our hearts pound. We breathe faster. Blood pressure rises. All this helps us fight or flee. But neither were useful options for the girl caught in the trap or the man bitten by the puff adder—or perhaps even for the hartebeest in the jaws of the wild dogs. If any hope for survival remains, slim though it might be, it may sometimes lie, against all odds, in remaining calm. How amazing to find that nature may afford us, even in the worst imaginable circumstances, a path to calm amid terror.

Afternoon: we spot another vehicle parked off-road. We drive closer to see what they're watching: five lions sacked out beneath a tree.

A wildebeest carcass lies fifty yards away. The lions face away from us, except for one, a young, maneless male, who rolls on his back, paws folded, revealing a belly stuffed with meat. Another lion rises, revealing the prominent nipples of a nursing female. Her cubs must be hidden nearby. She walks ninety-seven paces and lies down beneath a different tree. The others, females, lie on their bellies, except for one who is lying on her side. All eyes are shut, all lions are panting.

One grooms a paw, then licks her own back. The mother lion stands, repositions, and lies back down facing her sisters and brother. They are shaded by the tree. A breeze cools the sunny air; flies are few; water is near; their stomachs are full. It's a lovely day to be a lion here. Among them, we too luxuriate for a moment in their contentment.

But not for long.

"Oh, what *interesting* animals!" Dick says sarcastically. "Let's *do* stay and watch them!"

"I think we're going to move," Joshua answers sheepishly.

"I certainly hope so!" replies Dick.

It's been a splendid day watching animals, most of them healthy and happy. But the image of the wounded bulls and lost calves won't leave me. After the hot day, night offers us a chance to recuperate. But what about the wildebeests? I wonder: *Where do they sleep?*

Dick tells us they lie in "bedding formations" after a nighttime feeding peak, during which time they ruminate for several hours, coughing up the cud from the first part of the four-chambered stomach to chew it to extract more nutrients. "Ruminants don't really sleep," Dick tells us. Giraffes are the most serious insomniacs of the Serengeti; except for the infants, who lie down with legs folded, giraffes sleep standing up, often with one eye open, in short bursts that total only about thirty minutes a night. But other ruminants can't afford to sleep long, either. Because of their special stomachs, "they can't lie on their sides as zebras can," Dick explains. "They must lie on their breastbone to allow their digestion to work."

But they do rest—and they do nap. "An interesting thing about their brains," Dick continues, "is that wave patterns taken of resting ruminants are very similar to those of sleeping humans."

I am comforted to know they can rest, even without sleeping. How wondrous! The world may be kinder than it sometimes seems.

To close our day, I want to see wildebeests at peace. I want to peek in on their repose, the same way you might want to rest your loving gaze on a sleeping dog or cat or child. So at nine p.m., while Dick takes an early bedtime to recover from his cold, and while Anna packs her stuff to leave us to return to her job in Arusha in the morning, Logan, Liz, Roger, Gary, and I join four staffers from our camp on a night drive.

It's a great chance to see some of the small, nighttime hunters that most tourists miss: Genets, climbing, spotted, cat-like carnivores related to mongooses. Bush babies, primitive primates smaller than squirrels with enormous, forward-

Bush babies, primitive primates, are most active at night.

facing eyes. Both are treetop acrobats, most active after dark. We spot the eyeshine of a lone hyena, and then two black-backed jackals, out hunting.

And then, our car's headlights startle a male wildebeest. A camp staffer shines his powerful spotlight on the fellow. He limps away from the light. His back leg is broken. "Let's leave him be," we tell our guide—but he doesn't under-stand our English and thinks we want a better look. He tracks the wounded animal with the light, disturbing him further.

"Let's go on!" Roger suggests, gesturing forcefully. Now our driver understands, and he turns off the road. Birds called nightjars fly like Halloween ghosts through our light. We surprise five roosting shrikes—predatory song-birds—and spot two bat-eared foxes. The foxes are hunting for night-active insects. Jackals are hunting the African hares we see bouncing everywhere.

And then our guide illuminates another limping wildebeest. The spotlight finds the source of his injury: a broken right front hoof. The light licks up his body from the leg, and we see, with horror, that his shoulder is streaming with blood. This is the sort of injury a lion or a leopard would leave. But somehow, even with the hoof injury, this brave fellow escaped.

By now it's nearly eleven p.m., and we turn back to the road leading to camp. We're still scanning the trees with the spotlight when, just outside the gate to our camp compound, about twenty-five feet off the ground, we see a long, slender leg, a delicate ankle—and an unmistakable hoof. The corpse of a young wildebeest is cradled in the embrace of two of the tree's big branches. With Liz's light-gathering binoculars we can see the wound at the neck, streaming blood. A leopard killed it this very night, cached it in the tree, and will return to eat it later.

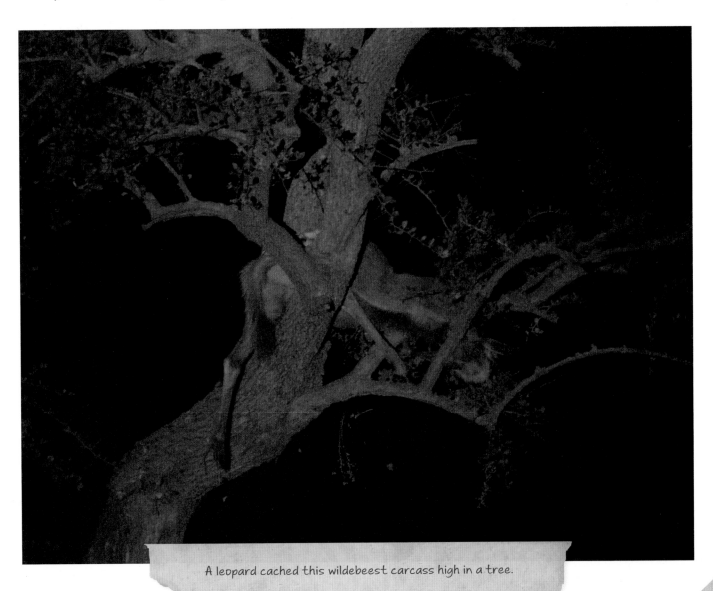

A leopard cached this wildebeest carcass high in a tree.

Other Magnificent Migrants: Zooplankton

MOST MIGRATIONS HEAD EAST OR WEST, NORTH OR SOUTH. THIS ONE HEADS up and down. And while migrations usually take place over months or more, this one happens once every day. It's the most massive migration on earth, yet it involves some of the smallest animals alive.

Every day, all over the world's oceans, a billion tons of tiny, floating sea organisms called zooplankton—many of them shrimp-like creatures called copepods two-tenths of an inch long or smaller—make their way to deep water in the morning, and then rise toward the surface as the sun sets. This process is called diel vertical migration. It has fascinated people ever since humans went to sea.

Mini-migrant: copepod, greatly magnified.

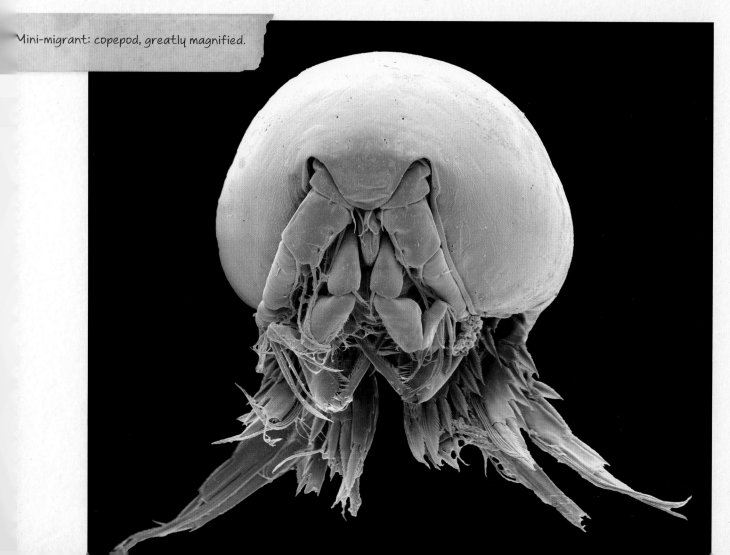

A billion tons of zooplankton migrate from the depths to the seas' surface each night

Why do they do this? How do they know when and where to go?

Scientists reason it's because these small animals are balancing the tradeoffs between eating tasty plant plankton at the ocean's surface and getting eaten by predators themselves while they're there. They face less risk of being spotted if they ascend toward the surface at night. So they hide in the depths by day and time their ascent for when it's dark.

But here's a mystery: even deep-sea zooplankton, who live in the inky depths, also make a vertical migration at night—even though they never come remotely near the surface. Yet they still follow the rhythm of a sun they can't see. Why—and how?

Are deep-sea zooplankton sensing the wiggly movements of millions of zooplankton above them and responding to that? Do these tiny animals have a precise internal clock that tells them when and where to migrate, like some birds and turtles appear to? And why would this benefit them, if they live in a world with no light anyway?

Though zooplankton are some of the most abundant animals in the world, they are also among the most mysterious. And they are also surely among the most important. They are just one rung above the plants at the very base of the ocean's food chain. They feed everyone from fish to birds to whales—and in this way, along their daily travels up and down in the water column, they keep the world alive.

Chapter Ten

"Our next stop is quite remote," Dick tells us as we pile into the car the next morning. Tonight we'll arrive at the last camp of our journey, where we'll spend our final three nights in the Serengeti. This is our concluding, best chance to journey among the migrating herds of wildebeests. "On the way, we'll search along the Mara River. And if the wildebeests are not there, we'll search Kogatende. If we're really lucky, there will be masses of wildebeests up north."

We leave the Ikoma Wildlife Management Area and reenter Serengeti National Park—a very slow process because the management has, for some reason, added computers to the already laborious paperwork rather than replacing it—and the computers are down. But as we wait at

Kopjes dot the landscape.

a little picnic area outside the gate to the park, Dick still finds drama to narrate: "Look—two robin chats are fighting!" The two red-breasted birds leap into the air from the dusty ground, lunging at each other. "There's terrific competition for territory, especially outside camps." Where there are people, there's food.

The delay at park HQ guarantees today's drive will be long and hot. We don't get moving again till eleven—at which point most of the animals have sensibly sought shade. We see few creatures but vultures and eagles; the landscape looks like an endless expanse of yellow, olive, and brown. The thorn trees by the road are coated with red dust. Spiny trees, burnt ground, yellow grass: the European foreigners who colonized this place, Dick tells us, called this kind of space MAMBA—mile after mile of bloody Africa. "But we call it 'mile after mile of blessed Africa'!" Dick says.

All of us agree. This is a patient, knowing, ancient landscape. In the absence of mammals, the trees seem thoughtful, even emotional. The branches look like strong arms. Are they holding up the skies? Is that why the tops of some of these acacias are flat, squashed by heaven's weight? Are the trees imploring the clouds for rain?

If so, the answer, today, is no.

As we sit quietly in the car, the land itself seems to whisper. Something important happened here. Of course, humankind arose in East Africa, but that, to me, is no more or less important than the other events this land remembers. Rain came, or it didn't. Elephants came through—or stayed away. Fires burned and burned out. Wildebeests horned the bushes and trees—or didn't.

The acacias here are all the same size, Dick notes. That's a testament to the rains that let them all grow, the animals who chose not to nibble them as seedlings and saplings, and the herds whose manure fed them when they were older. As we've learned to read some of the animals' behavior, we can now see, too, the his-

A klipspringer, the only antelope species that can live on kopjes.

tory recorded in the trees.

Soon we cross into a greener area. Dick describes the habitat as "woodland interspersed with these *beautiful* open plains." Many people would think the empty plains boring. But Dick thinks like a wildebeest. To them, nothing is lovelier than miles and miles of delicious, nourishing grass.

"It's still green here, but look at how short the grass is!" says Dick. At 2:05 we spot some females and calves with a bull beneath a tree, but the clipped grass means one thing: "The migration has come through here fairly recently. We could be seeing them this afternoon."

Now we're coming to an area famous for its many kopjes and for the only antelope that lives on these rocky hills: the sturdy little spike-horned klipspringer. Standing only twenty inches tall, it bounds up and down the steep slopes jumping from rock to rock, landing with all four feet together on the flat tips of its hooves. "Once," Dick tells Joshua, "your uncle and I counted one hundred klipspringers in this range of rocky hills!"

It's a thrilling habitat to explore, but the rocky track is tough on the Land Cruiser. We stop the car to check the tires and discover the left rear is low. Joshua changes the tire, and without the noise of the motor, we hear birds aptly named babblers chattering from the trees, as if arguing with one another, and the gushing notes of the magpie shrike. It sounds like a musical waterfall.

Dick wonders aloud whether we should proceed along this rocky track. There's a smoother road that eventually leads to our last camp, a bit to the west. But the rougher road, heading east, winds through a wild, beautiful landscape, different from most of what we've seen before, with many more intriguing kopjes. Joshua, done with changing the tire, puts the vehicle into four-wheel drive and heads east.

Fifteen minutes later, at four p.m., we hear a loud *clunk*. We've hit a rock.

"It sounds bad," says Logan. He, Roger, and Joshua look under the car. Roger delivers the diagnosis: "The impact of the rock strike jammed the right rear wheel so hard that it broke the leaf spring. The axle was knocked backwards, so the drive shaft is broken as well."

Liz and I don't need the translation to know the car can't go anywhere. And we are quite literally in the middle of nowhere.

We brace the front wheels with rocks and Joshua jacks up the car so that he, Roger, and Logan can crawl under. At least they're in the shade. At four, it's miserably hot, and the sun beats down like a hammer. Liz insists on standing in the road behind the car to make sure the jack is perfectly straight and still holding. "I'm not taking my eyes off it," she says. If it lets go, our friends will be crushed—taking out the youngest and strongest members of our group. And if they survive, but cry out in pain, they will draw predators.

While Joshua tries to get cell reception to

Joshua, Roger, and Logan start work on our disabled vehicle.

call for help, Roger and Logan attempt to remove the broken leaf spring. The bolts holding it on won't budge. "It's really locked on there," says Logan. "But at least it's not stripping . . ."

Joshua's cell phone is showing there's a network, but his calls aren't going through. Thirty minutes pass. "How's it going, guys?" he asks Roger and Logan.

"It's a real project," says Roger, glancing at a bloodied knuckle. In the Wood household, no effort is considered a "real project" until it draws blood.

But the fix we're in could prove far bloodier if nightfall finds us outdoors in lion and hyena country.

"Do you have an emergency number?" Dick asks Joshua.

"Tanzania doesn't have an emergency number," he answers.

"Do we have a spare bushing?" asks Logan. Usually made of rubber, the bushing in a car's suspension system functions like the cartilage cushioning the joints of a human skeleton.

"No," Joshua replies.

And still there's no cell reception.

Joshua decides to head for a mountain about a mile away to see if he can reach anyone on his cell phone. Liz and I object. "You can't go there alone! There are lions, buffaloes, hyenas . . ." But he dismisses our concerns with "I'll be back in a minute," and runs off before Liz and I can follow.

"Better find a comfortable place," Dick advises the rest of us. "We're going to be here awhile." I walk with Dick to a shady spot beneath an acacia, where Dick wisely goes to sleep. Gary stands by looking manly, but feeling helpless. Liz remains steadfastly in the road, watching the angle of the jack.

I make sure people are drinking water, and ask the guys under the car to explain more about the underbelly of the crippled Land Cruiser.

Roger and Logan are still working on removing the stuck U-bolts. They patiently explain that these bolts hang over the axle, which is sandwiched between the broken leaf spring and the rear of the car. Leaf springs are composed of several thin strips of metal, called leaves, arranged one atop the other to form a single piece that's curved upward, rather like a smile. The curvature helps the springs absorb the impact from bumps.

While leaf springs long served carts and carriages, as well as the first cars, including the Model T, these days they are mainly used for spreading heavy loads over a large area. They're mostly found on heavy vehicles like trucks. On our Land Cruiser, they're crucial to its suspension system—the system that supports the weight of the vehicle and allows the wheels to turn from side to side for steering. The axle—the shaft connecting the pair of tires, which was knocked backwards when we hit the rock—is fixed to the middle of the springs. So the first thing that has to happen before the damage can even be assessed, much less repaired, is to re-

As the long day wore on, the MacGyvering continued.

move the leaf springs.

It's 5:10: "The leaf springs are out!" announces Logan triumphantly. "And there is a spare!"

"But we still have the bushing problem," Roger notes calmly. There is no spare bushing, and without it, the other components of the suspension system will fail.

To solve the problem, Roger and Logan are trying to channel Kelly, Roger's wife and Logan's mom. At this moment, she is in Seattle, rebuilding a 1967 Austin-Healey Sprite. When she salvaged it, the car was in such bad shape a tree was growing out of it. When she's not working on rebuilding the Austin-Healey, she works part-time at a local car repair shop, where

she's so resourceful that the guys call her "the Swiss Army Knife."

What, Roger and Logan ask themselves, would Kelly do? "If my wife can do it," Roger is thinking, "I can too!"

But we have even more immediate problems besides the Land Cruiser. Joshua, who disappeared an hour ago, still isn't back. We don't know where he went, whether he found cell reception, or whether somebody has eaten or gored him. The camp where we're booked is a two hours' drive away. It's unlikely they'll come looking for us. They wouldn't know which of the two main tracks to scour to look for us anyway. We are in a remote, untouristed area. It's very unlikely we'll encounter a ranger or another car—especially at this late hour.

Dick, still battling his cold, remains immobile under the tree. I often forget my friend is eighty-eight years old, but I remember it now. I check to make sure he's asleep, and not . . . Good, he's breathing.

And at 5:25 p.m., more good news: Joshua has returned. "I scared up some wildebeests and hartebeests," he tells us—but mercifully, no buffalo, leopard, hyena, or lion. He reports that he managed to reach his dad in Arusha, and asked him to locate and call the nearest camp to send a car to rescue us. But which camp that might be, whether it might have working phone or internet, and whether it might be working today, on a Sunday, is all unknown. In fact, we won't even know whether Josh's dad is able to reach anybody, or whether they can do anything, until—or unless—someone shows up.

It's looking like we'll be spending the night in the car. Before darkness comes, I advise we all find our flashlights and dig out our jackets from our luggage before it gets cold. I inventory the food and drink in the car. We have plenty of water, two Cokes, five cookies, and two pieces of licorice among us. We'll be hungry, but at least we'll be warm and safe in the car.

Logan and Roger continue to work on the bushing problem. Their effort to channel Logan's mom has succeeded: they've decided to build a new bushing from the fabric of the towing strap and some black electrical tape.

Sunset comes to our dead car.

The sun is a sinking red ball.

Though sunset comes in less than an hour and a half, we all remain optimistic. "You and I can watch the landscape for approaching leopards, hyenas, and lions," Liz suggests cheerfully.

"Which is what we'd want to do anyway," I say.

"Oh, perfect!" she answers.

Dick, meanwhile, has risen, refreshed, from his nap beneath the acacia. He's in good spirits. "Another advantage of the night is we can use lights to send out an SOS," he notes. "That'll make it easier for people to find us."

By 6:15 p.m., Roger and Logan are maneuvering the spare leaf spring into position, a tricky operation that also requires reconnecting the drive shaft. "The wheels may have splayed out when we hit the rock," notes Logan, "and could put stress on the repair." The assembly weighs about 150 pounds. But our friends are undaunted, and their calm voices beneath the car buoy our spirits.

"It's gotta come down a little."

"No, it's stuck."

"OK, let me tap it a little."

By 6:30, crickets are singing their evening song. Liz and Dick sit together by the road, seemingly as content as two old friends on front porch rockers, watching an ordinary sunset.

"You hear something?" Liz asks Dick.

"Is a car coming?"

"No, no, it's not a car . . ." Liz says.

"I hear it," says Dick. "It's an ostrich."

"In the distance, lions and ostrich sound very similar," Liz comments.

"That's a fact," says Dick calmly. "Indeed they do."

"It sounds like a lion to me," Liz notes. "Not far, but not near. Not yet."

The sun is a sinking red ball. A wind picks up—and it's now that we notice, on the horizon, the fires.

The wind is bringing the flames toward us. And while we do not particularly want to sleep in the open in a place full of nocturnal predators, even less do we want to be sleeping inside a metal box over a tank of flammable gasoline while a wall of fire approaches.

By 6:55, Logan and Roger are working by flashlight. Both ends of the leaf spring are reattached. Next they line up the U-bolts that hold it in place.

By 7:07, it is now dark and getting cold and—

"It's in!" Roger announces.

"Sweet!" replies Logan.

And then, we hear the sound of a motor in the distance.

A vehicle bearing the name Lobo Lodge has arrived. It belongs to a $500-a-night hotel complex built to service a wealthy, mostly Arab clientele of big-game hunters at a concession just outside the park. The car has space for only four people; the driver is no mechanic, and he has brought no spare parts. But he has something else Roger and Logan need: bright headlights—by which, in another hour, incredibly, they finish the job.

We pile back into the Land Cruiser and, escorted by the Lobo Lodge vehicle, head for our unexpected, luxurious rooms: Hot running water. Electricity. Even hair dryers!

But before we depart, Dick offers a few words of advice to Joshua: "Don't hit the rock again on the way out."

Night coming on as fires rim the horizon.
We couldn't sleep in the car that night.

Serengeti on Fire

FIRE IN THE WILDERNESS SOUNDS DANGEROUS AND SCARY. BUT FOR MANY grasslands, fire may be just as nourishing as rain.

Every dry season, starting in June, planned and unplanned fires sweep across the Serengeti. Animals can smell the smoke from a distance; most everyone except tortoises, ground-nesting birds, and broken-down vehicles can simply move out of the way. These quick, relatively cool fires kill young trees, but not old, strong ones. The flames incinerate the leaves of grasses and herbs, but not the roots.

Once the fire burns out, the ash feeds the plants, stimulating new growth. The nutritious postburn flush attracts grazing animals. That's because young, tender, rapidly growing grasses are particularly nutritious. And fire has other benefits, too. It denies cover to predators. It kills ticks and other parasites. Many animals benefit. People do too—which is why people so often set them.

"Man-made fire has been such a universal factor in savanna ecosystems for so long," Dick wrote in *The Gnu's World,* "it is often impossible to determine how much

A controlled burn in the Serengeti.

of the African savanna is the result of human impact." No major fire started by lightning has ever been recorded in the Serengeti, where rain follows lightning strikes so quickly any flames are soon doused. Some ecologists even claim that human-set fires actually created Africa's grasslands. Others say that's nonsense. They say that climate and soil conditions interact to produce grasslands, and that millions of years of grazing by hoofed animals is enough to keep them from growing up into forest.

Everyone agrees, though, that fires can dramatically improve conditions for migrating animals. So park rangers, too, got into the act. They intentionally set grasses on fire every year. But the timing, amount, and location of burns has varied dramatically. Researchers have guessed that in some years, fires burned less than 25 percent of the ecosystem; in others, 80 percent.

What's best for the animals? Scientists are trying to figure it out. Today, satellite images can accurately map the frequency and extent of fires. The Serengeti's managers strive to create a mosaic of burned and unburned pasture. They don't want to let the grasses grow so high that they'll burn too fast and get out of control.

But rangers are not the only people setting fire to the grasses. Farmers burn their fields, and these fires creep into parkland. Poachers and cattle thieves set fires too: it's an effective way to cover their tracks. And because nobody puts the fires out, both planned and unplanned fires sometimes end up burning more grasslands than anyone intended. In his surveys in 2012 and 2014, Dick found that human-set fires had destroyed much of the favorite forage of the wildebeests and their fellow migrants—almost entirely by mistake.

Chapter Eleven

We spend the next day in voluptuous luxury. The hotel is built into the side of a kopje swarming with delightfully tame hyraxes. Gary, Liz, and I watch them, while Roger and Logan swim in the pool, Dick repacks his gear, and Joshua sees to the Land Cruiser's repairs. Even though the day after tomorrow we must fly back to Arusha, we can't complain about losing a precious day of our safari. We're chastened by our brush with danger. We're grateful simply to be safe.

Late in the afternoon, the vehicle repairs complete, we head north to the last camp of our trip. Not far from the border where the wildebeests cross into Kenya, Matembezi is a simple, intimate camp with only six guest tents, set out directly on the plains. Its location shifts every few weeks, along with the movements of the animals, to offer its guests the closest proximity to the migration.

And it's here that we wake the next morning to a smoky red sunrise, for our last full day on safari.

We set out heading due east, toward the Mara River and its shallower tributary, the Sand River. We might even catch up with the great masses at the crossing—but it's a halfhearted hope. We reckon we used up all our luck not getting eaten by hyenas or lions when we were stuck. But we expect to see some wildebeests along the way. We can wish them, at least, a safe crossing, and a successful journey.

Rolling hills give way to flat pastures. Soon we come upon a group of about a hundred gnus clustered together, grazing on fresh, emerald grasses—a configuration Dick calls a feeding spread. After all the miles of dusty ground and hoof-churned paths and tawny stalks chewed to nubs, this carpet of green must feel like a banquet to the wildebeests. Dick can almost taste the succulent blades. "If I hadn't just had breakfast," Dick says, "I'd be tempted to join them myself."

We're delighted to be among wildebeests again, even if they're not in huge numbers. And we've caught them at a moment when they seem exceptionally active. As we slowly cruise by, we spot a bull on his stamping ground. He raises a cloud of dust when he stomps his hoof. Then he bucks, kicking up his back heels, his long, black tail flying high. "He's cavorting!" Dick notes with delight. The big fellow sweeps his head in an arc from head to tail, lashes his tail, then horns the ground. "That can be a threat," says Dick. It could be directed at any of several neighbors. About seventy-five yards away, another bull rolls on his territory, imbuing his coat with scent he deposited on his stamp. Not far from him, a third male stands tall on his mound and shakes his head. The bulls could be threatening each other—or they could just be showing off to the females. "Look at that bull advertising," Dick says of the first fellow, who is bucking again. "This is the best damn grazing you're likely to find in the whole ecosystem! He's in full rut for sure!"

We drive on, over another rise, past a clump of trees, and onto another plain. The grasses here are golden, and have been more heavily grazed. A herd of more than a hundred elands, many of them calves and youngsters, cascades down a hill, and we catch our breath at the sight. Then,

The carpet of green must feel like a banquet to the wildebeests.

in the distance, Logan notices they are being followed by . . . dots.

Dots who are all saying, "Neh! Noooo-ooooo!!"

We drive on, descending another hill, rounding a bend—and suddenly, the plains are covered with them. Wildebeests are everywhere.

The horizon ripples with their bodies. Their calls envelop us in an aural embrace. It's a choppy, chaotic sea of wildebeests, and like waves in the ocean, they are both near and far at once.

We are close enough to hear the grasses swishing against their slender legs, close enough to see their eyelashes, close enough to inhale their warm, slightly musky scent.

"It's the wildebeest immersion experience!" announces Roger.

"I think we now can say we have caught up with the migration," Dick declares.

And now we get to experience what even the most well-made television special can't show. A camera must focus on one scene. It can't

A lone bull advertises his territory.

capture the feeling of being not just surrounded, but almost absorbed into a crowd of animals all around.

Wildebeests sweep around us like a storm. They fill our senses: We feel them in the backs of our heads. The Big Hum thrums not just in our ears, but in our bones. We breathe in their scent and taste it in the backs of our mouths.

They are everywhere we look: Wildebeests with tall horns, wildebeests with blondish heads, wildebeests with long manes, wildebeests with wobbling lips. Wildebeests with broken horns, with short horns, with no horns. Wildebeests bucking, horning, racing. Calves trotting beside their mothers. Wildebeests coursing forward in lines fifteen animals wide. Wildebeests walking parallel to our track in single file. Wildebeests heading the opposite direction. Wildebeests are coming from the west and north and south. And most of them are heading to cross the river into Kenya.

By 9:49 a.m. we reach the shallow Sand River and stop here to watch the crossing. We all stand up, as if rising to give a standing ovation. Lines of trotting wildebeests snake down from the hills and pour across the river.

"It's a great sight," says Dick reverently. "A great sight."

"They've picked a good spot to cross," says Joshua. "Nice and shallow, with no crocodiles."

We're glad—for the situation can be quite different. Crossing the Mara River is another story.

The Mara River is deeply cut. Because of this, animals usually cross at traditional points—fords created and maintained by the migration. Even these traditional crossing areas are treacherous; but in August 2006, Dick filmed thousands of wildebeests and zebras crossing between fords, upstream of one well-known camp. Pouring down a bank at a canter, they swam across—only to find themselves confronted by a thirty-foot vertical wall of dirt and rocks. The barrier was broken by only a few slender footpaths, wide enough for only one animal. "Wet wildebeests struggling to climb the wall made it very slippery," he remembers. Many tried to turn back. "Chaos ensued as wildebeests trying to recross ran into the oncoming hoard of swimmers." Exhausted animals, especially calves, were swept downstream by the strong current. Dick estimates only one in ten animals made it to the top. The rest lay dead or dying, drowned or killed in the jaws of waiting crocodiles.

A month later, once Dick was back home in Peterborough, New Hampshire, he heard of a tragedy far worse. Ten thousand animals died in five or six days at a crossing downstream from a different lodge on the Kenyan side. No one came forward with an eyewitness account, and at first it was thought that the wildebeests had been swept away by a flood. But from photos of the aftermath, Dick determined it was almost certainly a huge, horrible accident similar to the one he had earlier witnessed.

Dick knew that area well. It appeared that the wildebeests were only slightly off course from a traditional fording spot. But here, dense vegetation blocked their view of the crossing; they did not realize until they were already swimming that they faced a steep, rocky slope on the other side. But once the wildebeests started crossing, like people racing out of a crowded stadium though a single door, thousands of others followed. "Few could make it to the top of the wall," Dick reasoned, "and those who turned back were caught in the melee swimming toward them." Dead bodies washed down the river and piled up against a bridge. The crocodiles grew so fat on the carnage that they lay immobile for days, and vultures stained the riverbanks white with their droppings.

Luckily, at the shallow Sand River, the wildebeests we're watching face no steep slopes, no rushing waters, no hungry crocodiles. They sweep past us. Occasionally one stops to drink, but mostly they keep moving, braiding five, ten, sometimes fifteen abreast. The line keeps flowing for forty-five minutes, unbroken.

Then, suddenly, they stop. "Something's

The wildebeest immersion experience.

bothering them," Dick says. He swings his binoculars and spots the trouble. "A Kenyan vehicle on the other side spooked them."

As if crocs, floods, and steep banks weren't enough, the migrants now face an additional hurdle. Tourists line both banks of the river, often so close to the animals they have to step between the vehicles. And sometimes, for reasons known to that particular animal alone, a wildebeest will take exception to an individual Land Cruiser, and everyone behind will stop or turn back—a situation that, with slippery mud and lurking predators, can easily turn deadly for the very animals the tourists have come to see.

On our side of the river, wildebeests are piling up like cars at a traffic light. We feel the tension mounting, the pressure of hundreds of bodies, the disquiet of hundreds of troubled minds. And these hundreds can easily multiply to thousands.

"They'll build up and build up . . . and then suddenly start walking again," Dick tells us. While serving as a resident naturalist at a Kenyan lodge some years ago, he was often asked to explain "stupid" behavior like this. "They're not stupid," he insists. Imagine how you would feel: except for mothers with their calves, everyone in the herd is a stranger. Unlike zebras, who travel in organized family or bachelor groups, there's no acknowledged, experienced leader everyone knows and trusts. Arriving at water, "nobody is prepared to take the first plunge," Dick explains. Instead, they wait, wondering

"Why me?" and essentially say to the strangers surrounding them, "After you!" "No, after *you!*"

The first wildebeest to cross is almost always a bull, Dick has found. Bulls are usually in the forefront in any dangerous situation—not because they are looking out for the herd, but because "males are the impetuous sex." They have no responsibilities to the other wildebeests. Being in the vanguard of the migration during the rut will also allow leaders to intercept more passing cows. "And sometimes, being the first to cross water is a good strategy. By the time the crocs notice, you may have already crossed."

But sometimes the wildebeests employ a different strategy. If they're with zebras, they'll let them cross first. Sometimes they'll even follow a lost calf who wanders ahead.

At 10:10, the wildebeest dam has broken. The snaking line starts moving again. At first the animals take a different "off-ramp" out of the river, up a steeper bank. But in a few minutes, the crossing resumes its previous route, full-speed. The line straightens out.

A calf, arriving at the opposite bank without his mother, realizes his predicament and re-crosses the shallow water, calling for his mom. "Nyeh!! Nyeh!!" When separated, mother and calf typically both drop out of the larger group and run back and forth calling for one another. When it happens after a crossing, both mother and calf almost always turn around, swim back, and reunite at the first shore. This is such an effective move that Dick calculates that an incredible 99 percent of lost calves reunite with their mothers!

But this calf is different. "He's misusing the reunion strategy!" Dick says in dismay. When he emerges from the water, he wanders past the shore, deep into the oncoming throng. A cow turns back from the water and follows him for a while, but then she disappears into the larger group. "If that were his mother," Dick says, "he'd dive for her udder and suckle." We try to keep track of the lost calf, but soon the sight of the little body is lost among the others, his voice drowned out in the cacophony. Though we can't hear him, perhaps his mother can.

Most of us are still looking for the lost calf

A wildebeest at rest.

when at 10:43 Logan calls out: "Look!" He points to a fork in the Sand River, a quarter mile downstream from the wildebeest crossing. Here, on an open plain, in broad daylight, a long and low-slung spotted cat with a thick neck, wide head, and long upturned tail pads brazenly across the sand of the shallowest stretch of the river. A leopard!

This is the species Dick calls "the embodiment of feline power and stealth." We shouldn't be seeing a leopard here at all. Leopards hunt at night. If you're lucky enough to see one by day, it will be resting in a tree. Even Dick takes his eyes from the wildebeests to watch, mesmerized, as the predator crosses the open plain.

Two minutes later, a second leopard appears, one far more slender. "The only way you'd see two leopards together would be a mother and cub or a courting couple," Dick says. These two are probably male and female, and they aren't after the wildebeests we're watching. They headed back toward another herd we observed earlier, away from the water.

What a morning! "It doesn't get better than this," says Roger.

Roger was right. We drove on to the Mara River. I didn't want to see wildebeests tumbling

It's rare to see a leopard by day, rarer to see one active—and rarer still to see two of them.

down slippery slopes, or wildebeests getting killed by crocodiles—and we didn't. We went to one of the famous fords, Crossing Point Nine, where wildebeests were massing. We waited in the heat for an hour, but they didn't cross. We watched files of wildebeests and zebras marching down from the hills. We waited, awash in their voices. Finally, worried that vehicles like ours might be delaying them, we left.

We spent the rest of the afternoon, into the evening, just being among them. They flowed past us as we took in the wonder of their journey. The last thing we wanted to do was stop them—especially after all they had given us that morning.

"Until we saw that carpet of wildebeests this morning," Joshua said, "I'd have said we'd missed it."

"And still, we wouldn't have been disappointed," I assured him. "Our first visit with the wildebeests in the Crater alone was worth it . . ."

Everyone else was eager to add their own

favorite moments, up to now:

"Watching the hyraxes."

"Not getting eaten by lions and hyenas!"

"Seeing those bull wildebeests sparring."

"When we came upon all those elands!"

"Dick," asked Gary, "you've been at this more than half a century. How does what we saw this morning compare, with all your years you've been watching wildebeests in the field?"

Dick turned to make sure all of us in the Land Cruiser could hear his answer. "I never saw a better crossing," he said, "in my life."

Epilogue

The next morning, we join another group of visitors in a fourteen-seater Cessna, headed back to Arusha. We fly over ostriches and topis, zebras and wildebeests, thorny green acacias and pale golden grasses. MAMBA, I think: miles and miles of beautiful Africa.

Our short flight takes us over an active volcano, Ol Doinyo Lengai. It last erupted in 2007—its magma, the molten lifeblood of the planet, remaking the world. And then, to our right, we see Ngorongoro Crater, the remains of the ancient, exploded volcano whose sides form the microcosm that introduced us to the Serengeti.

Its hugeness should be humbling. But as we fly over it, I feel, instead, a tenderness toward this great landscape that so awed me when I

Ol Doinyo Lengai, an active volcano.

first saw it only weeks ago. Though I behold the world's largest intact caldera, I feel as if I am looking into a fragile teacup I hold in my clumsy, human palms.

Our kind arose not far from here. Prehuman fossils from Olduvai Gorge established Africa as the birthplace of humanity. Just to the west, the famous Laetoli footprints preserve what was, at the time of their 1976 discovery, the oldest known evidence of our upright-walking human ancestors: the delicate, lonely imprints record the steps of a tiny group of small hominins—perhaps a man, woman, and child—as they walked across the rain-cooled ash of another volcano on a vast, empty plain 3.7 million years ago. A plain that, nourished by the eruptions of these volcanoes, would, once a year, teem with wildebeests and their migratory entourage.

We owe this place a great debt, we humans. We're but a recent species, a naked, hairless, hoofless, hornless, and, compared with the animals we have met on our safari, toothless and pathetically slow mammal. And yet we threaten the very existence of the Eden where we were born alongside the magnificent herds who were here long before us.

The entire Serengeti has never been more vulnerable. As humans eat away at its boundaries, this last of the world's remaining great savanna ecosystems has lost 40 percent of its original area since 1900. Poachers line the wildebeests' migratory routes with snares. Some have even proposed fencing a large section of the Seren-

geti plains. Others want to build a new road through it. These threats force us to contemplate "the end of a spectacle that allows us to appreciate what Africa was once like," as Dick has said. "It would be the final demise of the golden age of mammals."

"The whole world has a stake in keeping this greatest African savanna ecosystem alive," Dick wrote in *The Gnu's World*. The final words of his book are in capital letters: "SERENGETI MUST NOT DIE!"

If I return, I wonder, will there still be herds massing at the crossings? Will the calls of rutting wildebeests rock through the night like a cantering lullaby? I don't know. But I do know this: the wildebeest migration created and maintains the African savanna, the place where humanity was born. No matter where we humans disperse on our own migrations, we owe it to the gnus, and to all the other creatures we met on this trip, to keep the Serengeti whole. If we lose it, we deserve no second chance. We forfeit forever the spectacle and renewal of the world's most magnificent migration.

Shortly after we took off, tourists on our flight looked down and cried, "Oh! The wildebeest migration!" We swiveled our heads to see. But no, they were wrong. It was only bushes lining a dry river.

Stars over the Serengeti.

Acknowledgments

Many people contributed to the success of our safari and the creation of this book. Of course my thanks are due first to the friends who organized and experienced this adventure with me. Special gratitude is due to Roger and Logan Wood and to Dick and Anna Estes for sharing the arresting images taken on our safari. But I wholeheartedly thank everyone who appears in these pages—and many who do not, for without them, this book could never have been written.

They include: Dennis Rentsch, of the Frankfurt Zoological Society, for an enlightening look at poaching and the factors that drive this practice in the Serengeti; Wesley Gald, for an overview of the superb antipoaching work at the Grumeti–Ikorongo Reserves; Eric Winberg, for translating my interview with Abraham Saidea; Joshua's parents, Lisa and Mike Peterson; my assistant, Emily Taub; my beloved editor, Kate O'Sullivan; the splendid book designer, Cara Llewellyn; sharp-eyed copyeditor Megan Gendell; and ultimate agent Sarah Jane Freymann.

In addition to the people in our story, my thanks to the others who also thoughtfully read and commented on the manuscript: Selinda Chiquoine; Joel Glick; Rob Matz; Judith Oksner; and my husband, Howard Mansfield (who calls wildebeests "the Styrofoam packing of Africa" to irritate Dick, but who secretly admires them).

Of course my deepest gratitude goes to Dick and to the Estes family: Runi, Lyndon, and Anna.

Selected Bibliography

Brown, Don. *The Great American Dust Bowl.* Boston: Houghton Mifflin, 2013.

Croze, Harvey, and photographer Carlo Mari. *The Great Migration.* London: Harvill Press, 1999.

Dharani, Najma. *Field Guide to Common Trees and Shrubs of East Africa.* Cape Town, South Africa: Struik Publishers, 2002.

Estes, Richard D. *The Behavior Guide to African Mammals.* Berkeley: University of California Press, 1991.

———. *The Gnu's World: Serengeti Wildebeest Ecology and Life History.* Berkeley: University of California Press, 2013.

———. *The Safari Companion: A Guide to Watching African Mammals.* Rev. ed. White River Junction, VT: Chelsea Green, 1999.

Flores, Dan. *American Serengeti.* Lawrence: University Press of Kansas, 2016.

Martila, Olli. *The Great Savannah.* Rauha, Finland: Auris, 2011.

Matthiessen, Peter. *The Tree Where Man Was Born.* New York: Penguin, 1995. First published 1972.

Schaller, George B. *The Serengeti Lion: A Study of Predator-Prey Relations.* Chicago: University of Chicago Press, 1972.

Stevenson, Terry, and John Fanshawe. *The Birds of East Africa.* Princeton, NJ: Princeton University Press, 2002.

Thomas, Elizabeth Marshall. *The Old Way: A Story of the First People.* New York: Farrar, Straus and Giroux, 2016.

Get Involved!

Since its inception, at a time when Tanzania was a new nation more concerned with its human citizens than its native wildlife, the Frankfurt Zoological Society's main focus has been the conservation of wild animal populations in Serengeti National Park. Today it supports Tanzania's National Parks authority, TANAPA, and Tanzania Wildlife Research Institute, in training and supplying guards, funding research, building infrastructure, and sponsoring community programs. Read about their programs here: www.fzs.org.

Here's how you can support the Serengeti De-Snaring Programme: fzs.org/en/projects/serengeti-conservation/serengeti-de-snaring-programme.

The Singita Grumeti Fund carries out conservation and community programs, including reintroducing native wildlife, fighting poaching, and working with local communities to provide alternatives to illegal hunting in the Grumeti Reserves. Visit them at www.grumetifund.org.

Dorobo Safaris organizes sustainable trips with Joshua and his family to the Serengeti as well as other sites in Africa. Kids are welcome. To find out more, visit www.dorobosafaris.com.

Photo Credits

All photos by Roger and Logan Wood except for: Jez Bennett/Getty: 112; Raphael Bick /Unsplash: 57; Jeremy Bishop/Unsplash: 76; Ricardo Braham/Unsplash: 75; sutirta budiman/Unsplash: 116; Sian Brown, 104; Don Burroughs: 2; Lucy Chian/Unsplash: 42; Flavio Coelho/Getty: (textured paper background throughout); Paul Cowell/Getty: 45; Julia Cumes/Aurora Photos/Getty: 21; Anna Estes: 48, 51, 52, 63, 78, 84, 98, 103; courtesy Estes family: 8, 12/13, 149; Richard Estes: 22, 27, 29, 50, 65, 73, 93, 109, 142; courtesy Frankfurt Zoological Society: 111; Gary Galbreath: dedication page; Steve Gschmeissner/SPL/Getty: 124; Andrey Gudkov/Getty: 144/145; Alex Guillaume/Unsplash: 88; Andrea Izzotti/Getty: 125; Loops7/Getty: (tape throughout); Medical RF/Getty: 85; courtesy Marshall family: 6 (left); Matija Mestrovic/Unsplash: 31; Sy Montgomery: 6 (right), 7 (all), 11 (right), 100, 130, 132, 133; Eric Murray/Unsplash: 60; Nastco/Getty (water background throughout); Augustinus Nathaniel/Unsplash (sky background): 88/89; George Pachantouris/Getty: 66; courtesy Joshua Peterson: 11 (left); Ray Rui/Unsplash (grass background throughout); Chris Schmid/Getty: endpapers; Leez Snow/Getty: 121; Putsada Sriphet/EyeEm/Getty: 8/9; Volanthevist/Getty: ii/iii; Wexor TMG/Unsplash: 77; HADI ZAHER/Getty: 58

Index